D0918328

SCREENING AND EVALUATING
THE YOUNG CHILD

SCREENING AND EVALUATING THE YOUNG CHILD

A Handbook of Instruments to Use from Infancy to Six Years

By

LOIS E. SOUTHWORTH, Ed.S.

*Department of Child and Family Studies
and Agricultural Experiment Station
University of Tennessee, Knoxville
Licensed Psychological Examiner*

ROSEMARY L. BURR, Ed.D.

*School and Counseling Psychologist
in Private Practice
Former Director of Psychological Services
Sevier County Schools
Sevier County, Tennessee*

ANDREA EWELL COX, M.S.

*Department of Child and Family Studies
University of Tennessee, Knoxville
Child Development Specialist / Teacher Trainer*

CHARLES C THOMAS • PUBLISHER
Springfield • Illinois • U.S.A.

Published and Distributed Throughout the World by

CHARLES C THOMAS ● PUBLISHER

Bannerstone House

301-327 East Lawrence Avenue, Springfield, Illinois, U.S.A.

© *1980, by* CHARLES C THOMAS ● PUBLISHER

ISBN 0-398-04129-6 (cloth)
ISBN 0-398-04131-8 (paper)

Library of Congress Catalog Card Number: 80-18677

Printed in the United States of America
V-R-1

Library of Congress Cataloging in Publication Data

Southworth, Lois E
   Screening and evaluating the young child.

   Bibliography: p.
   Includes index.
   1. Readiness for school--Ability testing.
I. Burr, Rosemary, joint author. II. Cox, Andres,
joint author. III. Title.
LB1132.S63   372.12′6   80-18677
ISBN 0-398-04129-6
ISBN 0-398-04131-8 (pbk.)

INTRODUCTION

Screening and Evaluating the Young Child provides an overview of instruments that can be used with children from infancy to six years. It was designed for use by teachers and others involved in the important task of assessing young children.

The need for such a sourcebook has become more acute since the advent of federal and state mandates for preschool screening, which directly involve teachers in the identification of those children who because of their physical or developmental characteristics may need individual attention or special programming. These mandates are forcing individuals to make critical decisions about instruments to use in early childhood programs, although in many cases those charged with making the decisions have had little or no previous training in test selection.

Teacher training programs in general have not included courses in assessment techniques, in part because there is disagreement among teacher trainers regarding the validity of testing children at such an early age. Educators have expressed concern over the improper use of test scores, which they believe results in premature, inaccurate or permanent labeling of children. Those who have questioned the quality of preschool tests have decried the shortage of properly standardized instruments that take into consideration the special needs and characteristics of young children. For these and other reasons teacher educators have avoided recommending tests for teachers to use with preschool children. Consequently, teachers often are poorly informed about what instruments are currently available and have felt obliged to refer children to specialists for even the most preliminary assessment.

In cases where teachers have been directed or have wanted to screen the children themselves, without initially involving outside professionals, there has been until now no sourcebook designed to meet the *specific* needs of the preschool educator in search of an appropriate instrument. Reference books which include instruments that teachers can use with preschool children have also included tests that are (1) designed for use with other age levels, (2) intended to be used only with identified handicapped children, and/or (3) to be administered by clinicians such as psychologists or pediatricians.

This book represents an effort to simplify the process of selecting tests for use by teachers of preschool children. To that end, we have included only tests that can be administered by teachers or, if administered by parents or paraprofessionals, yield information that is useful to the teacher as he/she designs and implements programs for children from infancy to age six. Some tests that are appropriate for teacher use were excluded if our investigation indicated the test either (1) is not currently available, (2) is intended for use with handicapped children only, (3) is part of a program without which it is minimally useful, (4) is highly specialized or is too research-oriented to provide useful information to teachers, or (5) requires a complex setting or extensive mechanical equipment.

The collection of instruments described in this book is the result of careful scrutiny of nearly 1000 instruments collected by the authors, who come from diverse but related backgrounds in teacher training, supervision, assessment, research, child development, and school psychology. Collecting instruments during the late sixties and early seventies, for the authors as well as other interested professionals, involved attendance at seminars, short courses, conferences, workshops, and state and national meetings of various organizations. More recently, a growing number of publications list and report information on tests. Those that we have found to be most helpful are listed in the bibliography. Other sources that we have found to be useful are professional journals, test publishers' catalogs, and direct correspondence with authors and publishers.

Divisions of the Book

The book consists of two parts, *Part I: Individually Adminis-*

tered Instruments and *Part II: Group Admisistered Instruments*. Part I comprises the major portion of the book because we believe that evaluation of preschool children is best accomplished on an individual basis.

Part I

In an effort to facilitate preliminary selection of the instruments in Part I, we have assigned them to several categories. Any method of categorizing instruments is necessarily arbitrary, since there is no universally accepted system for classifying measures of human characteristics. Our own system was determined by sorting the tests according to title, purpose, and skills or areas of development assessed. The tests within a given category may vary widely with regard to scope, method of assessment (observation, direct assessment, parent interview, etc.), and use of results (screening for referral, program planning, individual remediation, etc.). A brief explanation of our categorization follows:

COGNITIVE. All the tests in this section are intended to evaluate general intelligence based on verbal concepts, reasoning ability, Piagetian constructs, achievement in basic educational skills, and/or verbal and academic achievement.

COMPREHENSIVE. This section includes tests of general development for a wide range of ages, some beginning at birth and continuing to adulthood. Each test evaluates most if not all aspects of development, including cognitive, personal-social, gross motor, fine motor, communication, self-help, and visual and auditory perception. Some of the tests in this section are designed for use as general screening instruments.

LANGUAGE/BILINGUAL. The language tests assess primarily receptive and expressive language. Some include items or subtests that measure auditory and visual perception or memory, or some very specific aspect of language acquisition, such as syntax. Most of the bilingual tests are designed to measure oral proficiency in Spanish and English, usually for the purpose of determining which language is more appropriate for initial learning.

MOTOR SKILLS. Motor skills are usually included as part of a more comprehensive test. A small number of tests are intended to assess only motor development. For that reason these tests are placed in this separate category.

READINESS. This section includes tests designed to determine whether a child has adequate skills to succeed in an academic program. These tests usually assess reading and number readiness. Reading readiness tests may evaluate oral language skills, spatial concepts, left-right orientation, visual and auditory skills. Most of the tests in this section are designed to be given just prior to either kindergarten or first grade.

SOCIOEMOTIONAL. These tests may be used to assess emotional stability as it relates to school success, self-regard or self-concept, social competence, and school-related behavior problems. The majority of instruments included in this section measure self-concept.

SPEECH/HEARING/VISION. Tests in this section are designed to screen for possible problems in articulation, visual and auditory acuity, and/or auditory discrimination.

VISUAL MOTOR/VISUAL PERCEPTUAL. Some of the tests in this section measure the degree to which visual perception and visual motor behavior are integrated. Others are limited to the assessment of the ability to discriminate and/or recall visual stimuli.

Part II

Group administered instruments consist of tests that are generally used only with children in kindergarten or early first grade settings. As previously indicated, we recommend individual assessment because we believe that group assessment is more likely to result in erroneous judgments about young children. However, we recognize that other educators may consider group assessment unavoidable or even desirable. For this reason we have listed and briefly described a number of the many available group administered instruments.

The tests in Part II are divided into four categories, which are described as follows:

COGNITIVE. Tests in this category are intended to measure intelligence or reasoning ability, general verbal ability, and achievement in reading, math and/or language.

PERCEPTUAL. The tests in this section measure visual perception, auditory peception, and/or visual-motor coordination.

READINESS. These tests assess prereading (knowledge of colors and letters, attention, language, comprehension) and reading skills, mathematical concepts, and/or perceptual abilities for the purpose of determining school readiness.

SOCIOEMOTIONAL. This section includes measures of pesonal and social adjustment, academic motivation, and self-concept.

A number of tests whose names may be known to teachers because they yield information that is pertinent to the screening or assessment of preschoolers have been listed in an appendix titled "Instruments Recommended for Use Only by Clinicians and Specialists." These tests are appropriate for use with young children but should not be administered by teachers because valid results and interpretation depend on highly specialized training.

How to Use the Book

For the most efficient use of the book in making preliminary test selections, we recommend that the reader follow the process described below:

1. Consider the "Suggested Guidelines for Selection of Instruments to Use with Preschool Children" following this Introduction. The guidelines are intended to help the potential test user recognize and more clearly define his/her assessment needs.

2. Study the "Format Used for Descriptions" at the beginning of each Part. This outline will help the reader understand how the information in the individual test descriptions is organized and thus facilitates the selection of instruments for initial consideration.

3. Use the Contents and the Index to locate the descriptions of instruments that appear most likely to meet your basic requirements. After reading the selected descriptions, eliminate the tests that clearly are not appropriate.

4. Order samples of any tests that appear appropriate at this point. We do *not* recommend the use of the test descriptions alone as the basis for decisions about large scale test purchases. Specimen sets are often available.

SUGGESTED GUIDELINES FOR SELECTING INSTRUMENTS TO USE WITH PRESCHOOL CHILDREN

1. Identify the purpose of assessment (e.g., program planning, individualization, need for referral, academic readiness).
2. Consider only instruments designed for use with the particular age group to be evaluated.
3. Keep in mind the personnel available for assistance in implementing the assessment (teacher aides, parents, volunteers, etc.) Note the training required.
4. Ascertain which methods of collecting information (parent interview, observation, direct testing, etc.) are most appropriate to your situation. Note the training required.
5. Note the time required for administration of a given instrument, keeping in mind the need to accommodate the short attention span of young children and your own time constraints.
6. Whenever possible, limit consideration to tests that are individually administered.
7. Try to select instruments that provide information about norms, reliability, and validity.
8. Consider whether the test results will be used to develop a remediation plan. (Some instruments provide or suggest remedial activities and others do not.)

CONTENTS

SCREENING AND EVALUATING
THE YOUNG CHILD

Part One

Individually Administered Instruments

FORMAT USED FOR DESCRIPTIONS

This section contains descriptions of 163 instruments. An explanation of the format used for these descriptions follows.

TITLE. Complete name of the test followed by subtitles and acronyms if used.

AUTHOR(S). Full names of major authors.

DATE. Year of copyright or publication. For revised tests, the date indicates which revision is described.

PURPOSE. As indicated by the test author and/or publisher. Where several purposes were stated by the author, one or two are given.

AGE RANGE. Age in years and months, age range, or grade level as stated by test author and/or publisher.

WHO CAN ADMINISTER. As specified by the test author and/or publisher. Where not specified, professionals or paraprofessionals who meet the author's stated or implied requirements for background, experience, or additional training are listed.

TIME TO ADMINISTER. As estimated by the test author and/or publisher. Where no estimates have been made, as in the case of most rating scales and checklists, this is indicated by the term "unspecified."

DESCRIPTION. This section generally includes the following information:

Areas of functioning evaluated by the instrument

Item content, illustrated by examples or descriptions

Format of the instrument (length, number of items, design of test booklet, availability of alternate forms, etc.)

How the evaluation is conducted (direct testing, observation, interview, etc.)

Types of materials required and/or provided for testing

How scores are obtained and used

Format, length, etc. of the manual

Availability of supplementary materials (teaching aids, remedial activities, etc.)

Additional features of a specific instrument if the information seems pertinent to its usefulness or uniqueness

NORMS, RELIABILITY, AND VALIDITY. Availability of statistical information is reported as follows:

Manual Provides Information. The test manual contains rationale, descriptions, or tables of data compiled on norms, reliability, and/or validity.

Manual Provides Detailed Information. Significantly more information, usually in all three areas and with greater explanation, is contained in the manual.

Information Available. The manual does not include statistical information. However, the author or test publisher has indicated, either by direct correspondence or in some other publication, the availability of some information.

None Reported in Manual. There is no statistical information contained in the manual and we have found no indication that information is available from any other source.

None Available. This term is used when (a) the instrument is not normatively standardized, (b) test developers report that research is in progress, (c) no effort has been made to standardize the instrument, or (d) test developers indicate that they did not attempt to standardize because they consider the instrument to be criterion-referenced.

SOURCE. Name and address of publisher, distributor, or individual from which the instrument can be ordered.

APPROXIMATE COST. A dollar figure to help the user estimate the *approximate* expenditure involved in obtaining the basic test materials. Although this figure is based on current price information, it should not be used to order tests.

COGNITIVE

Albert Einstein Scales of Sensori-Motor Development: Object Permanence

AUTHORS: Harvey H. Corman and Sibylle K. Escalona
DATE: 1969
PURPOSE: To assess sensori-motor intelligence as reflected by stages in the acquisition of object permanence
AGE RANGE: 5 to 24 months
WHO CAN ADMINISTER: An examiner or teacher who has read instructions and who is experienced in infant testing
TIME TO ADMINISTER: 30 minutes
DESCRIPTION: The test is based on Piaget's theory of cognitive development and consists of a series of tasks designed to assess the child's continued awareness of objects removed from view (**EX:** Examiner holds toy slightly above eye level of child and then observes eye movement of child when the toy is dropped). There are 18 items on the scale, which is scored by a second person working with the examiner. Standardized equipment is not required. The manual describes common objects to be used. Detailed instructions for administration and scoring are provided in the 11-page duplicated manual; scoring criteria are also described on the score sheet.
NORMS, RELIABILITY, VALIDITY: Information available
SOURCE: Sibylle K. Escalona, Rose Fitzgerald Kennedy Center for Research in Mental Retardation and Human Development, Albert Einstein College of Medicine, Yeshiva University, Eastchester Road and Morris Park Avenue, Bronx, New York 10461
APPROXIMATE COST: Available from the above source on request

Albert Einstein Scales of Sensori-Motor Development: Prehension

AUTHORS: Harvey H. Corman and Sibylle K. Escalona

7

DATE: 1969
PURPOSE: To assess sensori-motor intelligence, as reflected by grasping, manipulating, and regarding objects
AGE RANGE: 2 to 8 months
WHO CAN ADMINISTER: An examiner or teacher who has read instructions and who is experienced in infant testing
TIME TO ADMINISTER: 30 minutes
DESCRIPTION: The test is based on Piaget's theory of cognitive development and consists of a scale of 15 observable behaviors (grasping of objects within reach, putting objects in mouth, putting hand in mouth, focusing on objects and grasping at them, etc). Common objects (rattles, small rubber toys, balls of colored yarn, etc.) are used to elicit the infant's responses and are described in the 8-page, duplicated manual, which provides explicit instructions for administration and scoring. The score sheet also contains brief descriptions of criterion behaviors.
NORMS, RELIABILITY, VALIDITY: Information available
SOURCE: Sibylle K. Escalona, Rose Fitzgerald Kennedy Center for Research in Mental Retardation and Human Development, Albert Einstein College of Medicine, Yeshiva University, Eastchester Road and Morris Park Avenue, Bronx, New York 10461
APPROXIMATE COST: Available from the above source on request

Albert Einstein Scales of Sensori-Motor Development: Space

AUTHORS: Harvey H. Corman and Sibylle K. Escalona
DATE: 1969
PURPOSE: To assess sensori-motor intelligence as reflected by stage achieved in the acquisition of spatial relationships
AGE RANGE: 5 to 25 months
WHO CAN ADMINISTER: An examiner or teacher who has read instructions and who is experienced in infant testing
TIME TO ADMINISTER: 30 minutes
DESCRIPTION: The test is based on Piaget's theory of cognitive development and consists of a scale of 20 tasks that require problem solving related to construction of objects in space (**Ex:** Examiner presents child with 2 or 3 blocks, demonstrates tower building and encourages child to do the same). The score sheet

contains descriptions of behaviors which constitute each level of development. Detailed instructions for administration are provided in the 14-page duplicated manual. The manual describes furnishings and common objects needed to administer the test.

NORMS, RELIABILITY, VALIDITY: Information available

SOURCE: Sibylle K. Escalona, Rose Fitzgerald Kennedy Center for Research in Mental Retardation and Human Development, Albert Einstein College of Medicine, Yeshiva University, Eastchester Road and Morris Park Avenue, Bronx, New York 10461

APPROXIMATE COST: Available from the above source on request

Basic Concept Inventory

AUTHOR: Siegfried Engelmann

DATE: 1967, Field Research Edition

PURPOSE: To assess the child's knowledge of beginning, academically related concepts

AGE RANGE: Preschool to 10 years

WHO CAN ADMINISTER: Classroom teacher or a trained examiner, preferably the teacher if results are to be used as the basis for remedial instruction and a trained examiner if results are to be used for special treatment or placement

TIME TO ADMINISTER: 20 minutes

DESCRIPTION: This inventory is primarily intended for culturally disavantaged preschool and kindergarten children, slow learners, and emotionally disturbed or retarded children. There are 21 items divided into 3 parts, which are described below with examples:

1. *Basic Concepts.* In the third item, the child is shown a picture, which is different for each item, and points or gives a Yes-No response to the request "Find the balls that are black (not white, big, not big, little and black, big and black)."

2. *Statement Repetition and Comprehension.* The child is asked to repeat a sentence and then to answer questions implied by the statement.

3. *Pattern Awareness.* The first item requires the child to identify a particular sound pattern as being the same or different from the stimulus pattern (slapping the table and clapping

the hands). The second item asks for repetition of digits, and the third evaluates sound blending.

In the teacher's manual the author discusses the differences between this criterion-referenced measure and the more familiar norm-referenced achievement tests.

NORMS, RELIABILITY, VALIDITY: None reported in manual
SOURCE: Follett Publishing Company, 1010 West Washington Boulevard, Chicago, Illinois 60607
APPROXIMATE COST: $20 for Manual, 100 Booklets, and 1 set of Cards

Bingham Button Test

AUTHOR: William J. Bingham
DATE: 1967
PURPOSE: To assess a child's knowledge and understanding of concepts and relationships he/she will encounter in primary school
AGE RANGE: 3 to 6 years
WHO CAN ADMINISTER: Teachers, and teacher aides, after a short inservice training period
TIME TO ADMINISTER: 30 minutes or less
DESCRIPTION: Test materials consist of 10 buttons of varying size, shape, and color in a plastic container. A total of 50 items are included with 10 items in each of the following categories: color, number, sizes and comparisons, object/object relations, and person/object relations. Each task requires the child to manipulate the buttons in response to the examiner's questions (**Ex:** "Show me the *white* button," "Put your finger on the *big* button," etc.). The author suggests that if a trained psychometrist or clinician administers this test, he/she can also observe visual and motor skill abilities of the child. Use of this test for children of higher socioeconomic backgrounds might not be suitable other than to make general estimates of ability. Instructions for administering and a record sheet for one child are in a 6-page manual.
NORMS, RELIABILITY, VALIDITY: Manual provides information
SOURCE: Bingham Button Test, 47211 North 125th Street East, Lancaster, California 93534

APPROXIMATE COST: $4 for Test Materials and Manual

Columbia Mental Maturity Scale (CMMS)

AUTHORS: Bessie B. Burgemeister, Lucille H. Blum, and Irving Lorge

DATE: 1972

PURPOSE: To measure general reasoning abilities and to assist those who need an indicator of developmental status for diagnostic and educational placement

AGE RANGE: 3-6 through 9 years

WHO CAN ADMINISTER: Educational and psychological personnel, classroom teachers, and others with practice and supervision

TIME TO ADMINISTER: 15 to 20 minutes

DESCRIPTION: The CMMS requires no verbal response and a minimum of motor response. There are 95 (6 by 19 inch) cards, each containing 3 to 5 pictorial and figural classification items. From 57 to 70 items are presented to the child, depending on age level. The administrator asks the child to point to the picture that does not belong with the others. There are 3 sample cards for practice. Total correct responses may be translated to an Age Deviation Score, Percentile Rank, Stanine, and Maturity Index. The 63-page manual discusses interpretation of these terms. Instructions in the manual are given in Spanish as well as English.

NORMS, RELIABILITY, VALIDITY: Manual provides detailed information

SOURCE: Western Psychological Services, 12031 Wilshire Boulevard, Los Angeles, California 90025

APPROXIMATE COST: $60 for Examiner's Kit which includes a Guide for Administering and Interpreting, 95 Item Cards; $5 for 35 Record Forms

Concept Assessment Kit — Conservation (CAK)

AUTHORS: Marcel L. Goldschmid and Peter M. Bentler

DATE: 1968

PURPOSE: To provide standardized assessment of intellectual

development as reflected by acquisition of the Piagetian concept of conservation

AGE RANGE: 4 through 7 years

WHO CAN ADMINISTER: Teachers who have studied the manual

TIME TO ADMINISTER: 40 minutes (15 minutes each for Forms A and B; 10 minutes for Form C)

DESCRIPTION: In a 26-page manual the authors provide a brief explanation of Piaget's developmental theory, directions for administration and scoring, a discussion of data from standardization procedures, and copies of the 3 forms used to assess conservation. Forms A and B include the following conservation tasks: number, substance, weight, discontinuous quantity, two-dimensional space, and continuous quantity. The first 4 of these tasks consist of 2 items each; the last 2 contain 4 and 5 items. Form C includes the area and length tasks; three items comprise each task. Printed beside each item on the recording forms are directions, verbal instructions, and response alternatives, as well as space for recording the child's explanation. For example, in Task II of the weight items, directions are given for the examiner to flatten one of two Play-Doh® balls into a pancake and then ask the child if the ball is as heavy as the pancake or whether one is heavier; the child is also asked to give the reason for his/her response.

NORMS, RELIABILITY, VALIDITY: Manual provides detailed information

SOURCE: Educational and Industrial Testing Service, San Diego, California 92107

APPROXIMATE COST: $27 for kit of testing materials, Manual, and one copy of each form

Expressive One-Word Picture Vocabulary Test

AUTHOR: Morrison F. Gardner

DATE: 1979

PURPOSE: To obtain a quick and valid estimate of a child's expressive verbal intelligence

AGE RANGE: 2 to 12 years

WHO CAN ADMINISTER: Teachers, psychologists, physicians, counselors, social workers, learning specialists and speech therapists (examiners should have studied the manual and should

be familiar with psychological and/or educational tests)
TIME TO ADMINISTER: 10 to 15 minutes
DESCRIPTION: In this test the child demonstrates his/her ability to understand and use words by naming pictures of single objects. There are 112 test plates, one picture to a page. The child names each picture as the examiner turns the pages of a flip book. Testing is started with the plate at the child's chronological age; instructions are given for establishing a basal age and a ceiling age in order that all items do not have to be presented. The raw score may be converted to mental age, deviation IQ, stanine, and percentile rank by reference to tables in the manual. The 32-page manual also includes a discussion of research background, test development, and statistical development.
NORMS, RELIABILITY, VALIDITY: Manual provides detailed information
SOURCE: Academic Therapy Publications, 20 Commercial Boulevard, Novato, California 94947
APPROXIMATE COST: $39 for Manual, Book of Plates, and 25 Test Forms

Grassi Basic Cognitive Evaluation

AUTHOR: Joseph R. Grassi
DATE: 1974
PURPOSE: To help identify basic cognitive deficits
AGE RANGE: 4-6 to 7 years
WHO CAN ADMINISTER: Teachers or others who have studied the manual or attended a workshop on administration (to be interpreted by clinicians, school psychologists, or other testing specialists)
TIME TO ADMINISTER: 20 to 30 minutes
DESCRIPTION: This instrument contains 29 items, which evaluate 10 areas of cognitive function:

1. Visual descrimination of colors, forms, sizes, and combinations of these
2. Basic concepts such as same-different and more-less
3. Naming of colors, numbers, and letters
4. Directional orientation of numbers, letters, and words
5. Visualization of a whole from its parts

6. Numerical concepts and quantities
7. Auditory discrimination of likenessess and differences
8. Kinesthesia (reproducing geometric forms)
9. Auditory and visual sequencing of forms, numbers, and letters
10. Visual and auditory recall of forms, numbers, and letters

For each area sampled, the manual and an informational booklet include a discussion of the rationale involved. Scores are translated to a Basic Learning Quotient, and it is recommended the Stanford-Binet Mental Age be used to obtain this quotient. However, the author indicates that a vocabulary score based on parts of the Grassi test might be used. A remedial training program is available that uses electronic apparatus and sequential programming.

NORMS, RELIABILITY, VALIDITY: Manual provides information
SOURCE: Dr. Joseph R. Grassi, 3501 Jackson Street, No. 110, Hollywood, Florida 33021
APPROXIMATE COST: $25 for Test Manual and 50 Record Forms

Hess School Readiness Scale (HSRS)

AUTHOR: Richard J. Hess
DATE: 1975
PURPOSE: To evaluate intellectual readiness to enter school
AGE RANGE: 3-6 to 7 years
WHO CAN ADMINISTER: Teachers who have studied the manual
TIME TO ADMINISTER: 10 minutes
DESCRIPTION: The scale consists of 45 items divided into 12 subtests: Pictorial Identification, Discrimination of Animal Pictures, Picture Memory, Form Perception and Discrimination, Comprehension and Discrimination, Copying Geometric Forms, Paper Folding, Number Concepts, Digit Memory Span, Opposite Analogies, Comprehension, and Sentence Memory Span. Raw scores may be translated to a mental age equivalent and an intelligence quotient. A classification table is used to interpret scores in terms of Poor, Average, or Excellent predicted school progress for both prekindergarten and pre-first grade children.

NORMS, RELIABILITY, VALIDITY: Manual provides information

SOURCE: The Stoelting Company. 1350 South Kostner Avenue, Chicago, Illinois 60623

APPROXIMATE COST: $28 for Manual, 50 Scoring Forms, and testing materials

Peabody Individual Achievement Test (PIAT)

AUTHORS: Lloyd M. Dunn and Frederick C. Markwardt, Jr.

DATE: 1970

PURPOSE: To measure achievement in the areas of mathematics, reading, spelling, and general information

AGE RANGE: Kindergarten through adult

WHO CAN ADMINISTER: Professional persons in education, psychology, social work, medicine, and vocational rehabilitation who have thoroughly studied the manual (paraprofessionals may administer the test if carefully selected, trained, and supervised)

TIME TO ADMINISTER: 30 to 40 minutes

DESCRIPTION: The PIAT requires no writing, only oral or pointing responses. Test plates are contained in 2 easel kits. Test questions are grouped accoring to 5 subtests: Mathematics, Reading Recognition, Reading Comprehension, Spelling, and General Information. For each subtest, questions are arranged in order of difficulty and instructions are given for establishing the basal and ceiling levels so the child is tested only over his/her own range of competence. Scoring is carried out during administration of the test. The 105-page manual gives instructions for translating scores to grade equivalents, age equivalents, percentile ranks, and standard scores. This is done by subtests and by total score. A profile can be plotted on the front page of the test booklet, and results can be compared to the child's IQ score if this is known. A wide range of potential uses for the test are discussed in the manual.

NORMS, RELIABILITY, VALIDITY: Manual provides detailed information

SOURCE: American Guidance Service, Inc., Publishers' Building, Circle Pines, Minnesota 55012

APPROXIMATE COST: $41 for PIAT Test Plates, Manual, and 25 Individual Record Booklets

Peabody Picture Vocabulary Test (PPVT)

Author: Lloyd M. Dunn

Date: 1965

Purpose: To estimate verbal intelligence through measuring hearing vocabulary

Age Range: 2-6 to 18-6 years

Who can Administer: Psychologists, teachers, speech therapists, physicians, counselors, and social workers who study the manual and follow all instructions

Time to Administer: 10 to 15 minutes

Description: The examiner's booklet consists of a series of 150 pages of black and white drawings. Each page has 4 pictures; the examiner asks the child to put his/her finger on the picture of the word named by the examiner. (Other methods for indicating a choice may be worked out for seriously handicapped children.) The words become increasingly difficult, but instructions are given for establishing the basal and ceiling level so the test is administered over only the child's range of competence. Separate instructions are given for administering the test to children below 8 years of age. The total raw score is converted to the child's estimated mental age, intelligence quotient, and percentile by reference to the appropriate table in the manual based on chronological age. The test record form includes a checklist for the examiner to note 10 types of test behavior (rapport, guessing, perseveration, etc.) and 6 physical characteristics (motor activity, speech, hearing, etc). These are rated on a 3-point scale. Test construction and extensive research findings are discussed in the 51-page manual.

Norms, Reliability, Validity: Manual provides detailed information

Source: American Guidance Service, Inc., Publishers' Building, Circle Pines, Minnesota 55014

Approximate Cost: $15 for Series of Plates, Manual, 50 Individual Test Records (25 Form A and 25 Form B)

Schenectady Kindergarten Rating Scales (SKRS)

Authors: W. Glenn Conrad and Jon Tobieson

DATE: 1969

PURPOSE: To measure important demensions of behavior that are related to future school achievement and emotional adjustment

AGE RANGE: 3 to 5 years

WHO CAN ADMINISTER: Teachers who have worked with their classes for at least 3 months, who are thoroughly familiar with the scales, and who have observed the child for a week or more with the scales in mind (to be interpreted by school psychologists)

TIME TO ADMINISTER: 10 minutes per child

DESCRIPTION: The SKRS consists of a battery of 13 behavior rating scales. Each scale contains 5 to 7 descriptions, which the teacher uses as criteria for rating the child's behavior. The behaviors to be rated are —

1. Waiting and Sharing
2. Level of Organization of Play Activities
3. Clarity of Speech
4. Use of Materials
5. Restraint of Motor Activity
6. Cooperation with Adults
7. Verbal Skills
8. Fearfulness
9. Frequency of Anger Toward Adults
10. Use of Scissors
11. Type of Motor Activity
12. Activity versus Passivity of Speech
13. Frequency of Anger Toward Children

Some items are scored according to frequency of the behavior, while others are scored in terms of the skill level of the child. For example, the scoring for "Use of Scissors" ranges from 1 for "This child has trouble holding scissors and cannot make a clean cut. The paper is usually crumpled or torn between the blades of the scissors," to a score of 5 for "This child cuts easily and can follow the lines closely even when the pattern is intricate." The Answer Sheet provides a profile of the child's scores, and the manual discusses the classification and interpretation of these profiles.

NORMS, RELIABILITY, VALIDITY: Manual provides information

SOURCE: Educational Testing Service, Princeton, New Jersey 08540

APPROXIMATE COST: Available from above source

Slosson Intelligence Test (SIT) for Children and Adults

AUTHOR: Richard L. Slosson
DATE: 1963
PURPOSE: To provide quick individual intelligence screening for children and adults
AGE RANGE: 4 into adulthood
WHO CAN ADMINISTER: Teachers, principals, psychometrists, psychologists, guidance counselors, social workers, school nurses, and other responsible persons who in their professional work often need to evaluate an individual's mental ability
TIME TO ADMINISTER: 10 to 20 minutes
DESCRIPTION: There are approximately 200 items on the SIT, including mostly nonverbal items at the lower levels (**Ex:** "Can walk up and down stairs alone") and requiring mostly verbal responses at the higher levels (**Ex:** "How many months in a year?"). The test items are similar in nature to the Stanford-Binet tasks, and the Stanford-Binet was used in validation studies. The administrator is instructed to begin testing at the level where he or she thinks the individual can pass 10 items in a row and to continue until the individual misses 10 in a row. The 32-page manual includes the test questions, detailed instructions for test administration and scoring, and a discussion of test construction and validation. An "IQ-finder" in the back of the manual facilitates determination of IQ scores.
NORMS, RELIABILITY, VALIDITY: Manual provides detailed information
SOURCE: Slosson Educational Publications, P. O. Box 280, East Aurora, New York 14052
APPROXIMATE COST: $13 for manual and 20 Score Sheets

Stibal Piaget Kit

AUTHOR: Willard O. Stibal
DATE: 1971
PURPOSE: To aid in determining at which Piagetian level a child is functioning
AGE RANGE: 4 to 13 years

WHO CAN ADMINISTER: Teachers who have studied the instructions for administration, and paraprofessionals who have been trained to administer the instrument
TIME TO ADMINISTER: 18 minutes
DESCRIPTION: This instrument, which involves the use of props, consists of 8 Piagetian tasks: conservation of discrete quantity, length, area, mass, weight, volume, formal operations, and classification. Instructions and illustrations for administering each task are provided in a 4-page mimeographed scoring form and a 3-page mimeographed set of directions; props are provided as part of the kit. Scoring is both for the child's correct initial response and for additional explanations by the child of the processes involved. A summary shows points earned for each of the tasks and total score.
NORMS, RELIABILITY, VALIDITY: None reported in instruction sheets
SOURCE: Bureau of Measurements, Emporia State University, 12th and Commercial Streets, Emporia, Kansas 66801
APPROXIMATE COST: $9 for Instruction Sheets, Scoring Forms, and Materials

Wachs Analysis of Cognitive Structures

AUTHORS: Harry Wachs and Lawrence J. Vaughan
DATE: 1977
PURPOSE: To determine the appropriate level of activites for a particular child's development and learning experiences
AGE RANGE: 3 to 6 years
WHO CAN ADMINISTER: Assessment professionals, classroom teachers, and teacher aides who have studied the manual and have had general experience with individual testing
TIME TO ADMINISTER: 30 to 45 minutes
DESCRIPTION: The test, which is based on Piaget's theory of cognitive development, consists of 137 items grouped into 4 subtests:

1. Identification of Objects
   Color Identification, Visual and Auditory (**Ex:** Child visually matches same-colored blocks and identifies each as named by examiner)

Shape Identification, Visual and Auditory (**Ex:** Child visually matches blocks with identical geometric shapes and identifies blocks as they are named by examiner)

Hand Identification, Visual and Auditory (**Ex:** Child identifies shapes by investigating them only by touch following examiner's requests, such as "Give me one the same as this" and "Give me the square")

2. Object Design

Block Stacking and Block Construction (**Ex:** Child reproduces examiner's models)

Pegboard Figure-Ground (**Ex:** Child reproduces examiner's pegboard designs)

Formboards (**Ex:** Child places solid, split, and half forms in formboards)

3. Graphic Design

Form Reproduction, Auditory and Visual (**Ex:** Child follows directions to draw several designs and copies other designs)

Graphic Control (**Ex:** Child traces between and on lines, draws a person, etc.)

4. General Movement

Mental Map of the Body (**Ex:** Child lies on stomach and lifts arms, legs, or head on request)

Balance and Coordinated Actions (**Ex:** Child balances on one foot, hops, skips, catches ball, and walks line)

For some subtests, testing is discontinued after two failures. In addition to instructions for scoring and interpretations, the 67-page manual discusses the rationale for selection of test items and gives suggestions for supplementary diagnostic procedures. Materials for curriculum planning and an extensive bibliography are also included. Remediation material is available.

NORMS, RELIABILITY, VALIDITY: Manual provides detailed information

SOURCE: Western Psychological Services, 12031 Wilshire Boulevard, Los Angeles, California 90025

APPROXIMATE COST: $150 for Manual, 10 Record Booklets and Profile Sheets, and set of test materials

Wide Range Achievement Test (WRAT): 1978 Edition

AUTHORS: Joseph F. Jastak, Sidney W. Bijou, and Sarah R. Jastak

DATE: 1978

PURPOSE: To measure achievement in basic educational skills

AGE RANGE: 5 years and over

WHO CAN ADMINISTER: Professional and paraprofessional personnel who have carefully studied and understood directions for test administration (interpretation should be by psychologists or other trained evaluators)

TIME TO ADMINISTER: 15 to 20 minutes

DESCRIPTION: The WRAT measures achievement in word recognition and pronunciation, written spelling, and arithmetic computation. There are 2 levels: Level I for children 5 to 11 years and Level II for children 12 years and over. The 4-page test form contains both levels. For preschool children, testing involves the following:

1. *Spelling.* Child copies a row of 18 geometric-type designs and prints or writes name. Depending on proficiency shown by the child, the administrator then dictates words for written spelling.
2. *Arithmetic.* Child counts dots, reads digits, shows requested number of fingers, tells which of a pair of numbers is larger or smaller, and is asked several oral addition and subtraction problems. These items are followed by written problems of increasing difficulty.
3. *Reading.* At the prereading level, child is asked to name and/or match several letters of the alphabet. If successful at these tasks, the child then reads from a list of words of increasing difficulty.

Instructions for administration must be followed exactly as specified in the manual; for example, each subtest has a time limit. Raw scores may be translated to a grade level, standard scores, and percentiles by age. The 96-page manual discusses standardization, interpretation, theoretical considerations and test criteria for learning disabilities, approaches to teaching, etc.

etc.

NORMS, RELIABILITY, VALIDITY: Manual provides detailed information

SOURCE: Jastak Associates, Inc., 1526 Gilpin Avenue, Wilmington, Delaware 19806

APPROXIMATE COST: $14 for Manual and 50 Test Forms

Category 2

COMPREHENSIVE

Ahr's Individual Development Survey (AIDS)

AUTHOR: A. Edward Ahr

DATE: 1970

PURPOSE: To determine specific or multiple problems requiring special planning by the staff at the outset of the child's education

AGE RANGE: Beginning of kindergarten or beginning of first grade

WHO CAN ADMINISTER: Parents complete questionnaire after reading instructions

TIME TO ADMINISTER: Unspecified (questionnaire)

DESCRIPTION: This survey comes in a 5-page booklet to be completed by parents of the child being screened. The forms in the booklet elicit developmental, medical, and behavioral information about the child (prenatal history, labor and delivery, baby's condition at birth, medical history, and preschool experiences). The test author recommends that after the information is collected, it be reviewed by a team of specialists to determine the special needs, if any, of the child. Included is a page for notes, comments, and recommendations for school personnel to complete. The manual provides a summary of age levels at which children usually accomplish developmental tasks.

NORMS, RELIABILITY, VALIDITY: None reported in manual

SOURCE: Priority Innovations, Inc., P.O. Box 792, Skokie, Illinois 60076

APPROXIMATE COST: $10 for Manual and 35 Booklets

Bannatyne System: Early Screening and Diagnostic Tests (BS:ESDT)

AUTHOR: Alexander D. Bannatyne

DATE: 1975

23

Purpose: To identify children who may have some kind of handicap or learning disability (Phase One), and to obtain a profile of the high-risk child in terms of his or her strengths and weaknesses (Phase Two)

Age Range: 4 through 6 years

Who can Administer: Psychologists, or teacher with university credits in psychological or educational testing (specific training required for the BS:ESDT involves supervised administration and scoring with a variety of subjects)

Time to Administer: 15 to 25 minutes for Phase One; longer for Phase Two

Description: Phase One, Screening Assessment, consists of a questionnaire for the child's mother or guardian, an observation checklist for the examiner, and 5 tests. The 5 tests are described below:

1. *Symbol to sound.* Subject is taught to read several short words composed of familiar letter sounds with imaginary symbols such as "The symbol X stands for the sound /m/ as in meet."
2. *Tactile finger sensing.* The examiner touches 2 of the child's fingers. The child, without looking at his/her hand, points on a diagram to the finger between the 2 touched by the examiner.
3. *Pictorial mistakes.* The child is shown a series of pictures one at a time. Each of the common objects represented in the picture has something wrong with it that the child must identify.
4. *Sound. blending.* The administrator pronounces words very slowly so that the child hears only the sounds in the words. The child is asked to identify the word, such as "m-o-th-er."
5. *Coding speed.* The child is taught a code of symbols and asked to quickly memorize and then to write the symbols.

The author suggests that Phase One be administered to all children entering school at the nursery school, kindergarten, or grade one level and that Phase Two, Diagnostic Assessment, be administered to all those children scoring below the 40th percentile for their age group (or, for school districts with limited facilities, below the 30th percentile). Phase Two consists of the following tests: recall vocabulary, balance, design matching, auditory closure, form memory, auditory vocal sequencing memory, dexterity/parallels, spatial form recognition and echo words. The examiner's handbook contains a description of Phase One and Phase Two and general instructions for administration; detailed instructions for administering and scoring the individual tests are contained in the examiner's test administration booklet. Stimulus booklets are used for some of the tests. Phase One and Phase Two may be ordered separately.

NORMS, RELIABILITY, VALIDITY: Information available

SOURCE: Learning Systems Press, P.O. Box 2999, Lafayette, Louisiana 70501

APPROXIMATE COST: Available from above source

Barclay Early Childhood Skills Assessment Guide

AUTHORS: Lisa K. Barclay and James R. Barclay

DATE: 1976

PURPOSE: To identify target needs of young children

AGE RANGE: Preschool, kindergarten, and first grade

WHO CAN ADMINISTER: Teachers or aides who have studied the manual and who have observed the child's activities for 1 to 2 weeks

TIME TO ADMINISTER: Unspecified (checklist)

DESCRIPTION: The checklist includes 143 items based on observations (**Ex:** "Child can perform a simple task in sequence") of the following areas of functioning: Sensory Tasks, Motor Perceptual Tasks, Environmental Exploration, Visual and Auditory Imitation, Sensory and Memory Discrimination, Self-Concept, Attending-Responding, Task-Order Skills, and Social Interaction Skills. The Self-Concept portion must be administered orally to each child and consists of 25 items, such as "Are you nice to your friends most of the time?" A Parent Rating Scale is also included. The teacher asks the parent 10 questions about the child and rates the responses on a 4-point scale. Scoring on most of the items is in terms of Deficient, Needs Improvement, or Satisfactory. However, the Self-Concept Scale items are scored Yes or No and the total self-concept score is classified as Needs Help, Adequate, and Above Average.

A computerized version of the instrument is available, which provides group results for the class and individual interpretation for the child based on class norms. The 75-page manual includes discussion of intervention strategies. Additional teaching materials are available.

NORMS, RELIABILITY, VALIDITY: Manual provides information
SOURCE: Educational Skills Development, Inc., 431 South Broadway, Suite 321, Lexington, Kentucky 40508
APPROXIMATE COST: $11 for Manual and 25 hand-scoring forms. Cost of computer processing and reporting available from above source

Behavioral Characteristics Progression (BCP)

AUTHORS: Santa Cruz County Schools (Special Education Management Project)
DATE: 1973
PURPOSE: To assist in comprehensive assessment, goal-setting, record-keeping, and parent communications
AGE RANGE: 1 to 14 years
WHO CAN ADMINISTER: Teachers who have attended a workshop on administration of the BCP
TIME TO ADMINISTER: Unspecified
DESCRIPTION: The BCP consists of 59 Goal Areas or "behavioral strands," each of which describes up to 50 developmentally sequenced (rather than age-related) behaviors. Each Goal Area begins with primary behaviors (**Ex:** "Cooperates passively when being dressed") and ends with behaviors approximating appropriate adult behavior. Included in the 59 Goal Areas are, among others, self-help skills such as Feeding/Eating, language skills such as Articulation and Language Comprehension, motor skills, and personal characteristics such as Impulse Control and Honesty. Large charts (18 by 40 inch) may be used to show the child's performance across all Goal Areas simultaneously.
NORMS, RELIABILITY, VALIDITY: None reported in manual
SOURCE: VORT Corporation, P.O. Box 11132, Palo Alto, California 94306
APPROXIMATE COST: $18 for Charts, Binder, and Observation

Booklet; Spanish version also available.

Birth to Three Developmental Scale

AUTHORS: Tina E. Bangs and Susan Dodson
DATE: 1978
PURPOSE: To identify developmental strengths and weaknesses
AGE RANGE: Birth to 3 years
WHO CAN ADMINISTER: Teachers and other child development specialists who have studied the manual and gained experience with the scale by assessing at least 6 normal children
TIME TO ADMINISTER: Unspecified
DESCRIPTION: This scale assesses development in 5 areas of functioning. Two to three items for each area are grouped at 6-month intervals between birth and 3 years. The areas are Language Expression, Language Comprehension, Problem Solving, Social/Personal, and Motor. Typical developmental items are used; for example, at the 30 to 36 month level an item under Language Expression is "Can carry on a conversation," and an item under Motor is "Turns pages of a book one by one." Administration and scoring instructions are given in the 72-page manual. There is a separate scoring sheet for each of the 5 areas. A developmental age level is obtained for each area; these age levels may be plotted on a summary sheet for periodic reassessment.
NORMS, RELIABILITY, VALIDITY: None reported in manual
SOURCE: Teaching Resources Corporation, 50 Pond Park Road, Hingham, Massachusetts 02043
APPROXIMATE COST: $22 for Manual, 5 pads of Scoring Sheets of 50 each, and a pad of 50 Summary Forms

Boyd Developmental Progress Scale

AUTHOR: Robert D. Boyd
DATE: 1974
PURPOSE: To measure growth and development of children
AGE RANGE: Birth through 8 years
WHO CAN ADMINISTER: Child development specialists and clinicians

TIME TO ADMINISTER: 10 to 20 minutes

DESCRIPTION: The scale consists of 15 items that measure 3 areas of functioning: motor skills, communication skills, self-sufficiency skills. The Motor Skills section includes fine and gross motor activities; the Communications Skills section covers comprehension or cognitive skills and measures what the child can do by actual testing; and the Self-Sufficiency Skills section measures, through parent interview, what the child typically does. Behaviors are scored as present or absent. The entire scale, which contains 5 items for each of 10 age levels, is contained on a single page in order to facilitate comparison across skill areas.

NORMS, RELIABILITY, VALIDITY: Information available

SOURCE: Inland Counties Regional Center, Inc., P.O. Box 6129, San Bernadino, California 92412

APPROXIMATE COST: $9 for Manual and 20 copies of the Scale

Carolina Developmental Profile

AUTHORS: David L. Lillie and Gloria L. Harbin

DATE: 1975

PURPOSE: To determine developmental abilities in order to assist the teacher in establishing long-range objectives

AGE RANGE: 2 through 5 years

WHO CAN ADMINISTER: Teachers who have studied the profile booklet

TIME TO ADMINISTER: 30 to 40 minutes, to be given in several sessions

DESCRIPTION: This Profile consists of 83 items divided into 6 areas of functioning: Gross Motor, Fine Motor, Visual Perception, Reasoning, Receptive Language, and Expressive Language. Items for each area are grouped according to age levels (2, 3, 4, and 5 years) with 2 to 6 items at each level. All items are stated in behavioral terms. For example, a Reasoning task at the 5-year level is "Touches the middle in a row of five blocks on request. Present blocks half an inch apart in a row. Allow one trial." Scoring is checked Can Do or Cannot Do. The Developmental Age for each area is the highest age level at which the child can accomplish two or more tasks. Tasks that were failed below this level are considered to be long-range objectives. After these are mastered, the tasks immediately above those that have been passed become the next objectives. A profile sheet is used to summarize the information by Developmental Age for each area. However, the authors emphasize that these age levels are not to be used as diagnostic labels but as guides for setting up sequential objectives. The 15-page profile booklet includes a page of instructions and a bibliography on which test items were based. This instrument was designed to be used with a developmental task instruction system, which is available.

NORMS, RELIABILITY, VALIDITY: Information available
SOURCE: Kaplan Press, 600 Jonestown Road, Winston-Salem, North Carolina 27103
APPROXIMATE COST: $.60 each for 20 or more of the Profile Booklets

Child Development Assessment Form: Birth to Three

AUTHORS: Marsha Kaufman and T. Thomas McMurrain
DATE: 1979
PURPOSE: To help the teacher observe the child in different areas of development and to follow changes
AGE RANGE: Birth to 3 years
WHO CAN ADMINISTER: Parents and teachers who have read the instructions
TIME TO ADMINISTER: Unspecified (checklist)
DESCRIPTION: A checklist of skills and behaviors that a child is likely to develop between birth and 3 years is scored after observing the child in everyday play and work activities over a period of time. The following areas, with 18 items for each, are surveyed: Social-Emotional (**Ex:** "Focuses attention on face of another person"), Language (**Ex:** "Laughs out loud"), Cognitive (**Ex:** "Carries object in hand to mouth"), Gross Motor (**Ex:** "Holds head and chest up while lying on stomach"), Fine Motor (**Ex:** "Holds rattle placed in hand"). In completing the checklist, the administrator distinguishes between behaviors that are not firmly mastered and those that are. Space is provided in the 12-page record booklet for recording observations 3

times during the year. A summary profile chart is provided.
NORMS, RELIABILITY, VALIDITY: None available
SOURCE: Humanics Associates, 881 Peachtree Street, N. E., Atlanta, Georgia 30309
APPROXIMATE COST: $.50 for each form

Child Development Assessment Form: Ages Three to Six

AUTHORS: T. Thomas McMurrain and Fan Brooke
DATE: 1975
PURPOSE: To assist teachers in observing areas of development and to plan educational activities for the child
AGE RANGE: 3 to 6 years
WHO CAN ADMINISTER: Parents and teachers who have read the instructions
TIME TO ADMINISTER: Unspecified (checklist)
DESCRIPTION: A 64-item checklist of skills and behaviors a child is likely to develop during the ages 3 to 6 is scored over a period of time after observing the child in everyday play and work activities. The following areas are surveyed: Cognitive (**Ex:** "Identifies body parts"); Social-Emotional (**Ex:** "Interacts with children"); Motor Skills (**Ex:** "Copies a circle"); Hygiene and Self-Help (**Ex:** "Recognizes toilet needs"). In completing the checklist, the teacher distinguishes between behaviors that are not firmly mastered and those that are. A planning sheet that specifies areas of improvement, problem areas, and follow-up activities planned for the child is included. There is also a summary profile sheet. The authors stress that the checklist is not a normative instrument and should not be used to compare one child with another.
NORMS, RELIABILITY, VALIDITY: None available
SOURCE: Humanics Associates, 881 Peachtree Street, N. E., Atlanta, Georgia 30309
APPROXIMATE COST: $.50 for each form

Childhood Identification of Learning Disabilities (CHILD): Screening and Diagnostic Materials

AUTHORS: Developed by the Westinghouse Learning Corporation

DATE: 1974

PURPOSE: To provide for early identification and diagnosis of children with learning disabilities in order that early treatment may be provided

AGE RANGE: Kindergarten through third grade

WHO CAN ADMINISTER: Teachers who have studied the manual, paraprofessionals under supervision, and psychologists

TIME TO ADMINISTER: 20 to 30 minutes for each form

DESCRIPTION: The initial component of CHILD is the Early Identification Screening Inventory, which consists of 100 items that screen 6 areas of behavior: visual motor, visual, speech and hearing, physical and behavior, psychomotor, and psychological. The teacher marks Yes or No for each item; results provide a preliminary ranking of students. Three additional instruments, may be obtained separately:

1. Motor Perceptual Diagnostic Inventory (gross motor control, balance and coordination, neural maturity, ocular motility, and eye/hand dominance)
2. Fine Visual and Motor Screening Inventory (fine motor control, left-to-right orientation, perceptual and spatial organization, attention to visual detail, closure ability, size discrimination, and head and eye orientation)
3. Perceptual Organization Screening Inventory (visual perception, directionality, perceptual organization, form Gestalt, and ability to follow verbal instructions)

The complete CHILD program includes, in addition to the above materials, a prescriptive programming component and a curriculum series based on findings from the screening and diagnostic processes. Training programs are available.

NORMS, RELIABILITY, VALIDITY: Manuals provide information

SOURCE: Westinghouse Learning Corporation, 5005 West 110th Street, Oak Lawn, Illinois 60453

APPROXIMATE COST: $10 for complete materials for each of the three diagnostic inventories ($120 for the complete CHILD Program)

Cognitive Skills Assessment Battery

AUTHORS: Ann E. Boehm and Barbara R. Slater

DATE: 1974

PURPOSE: To provide through systematic assessment a profile of competencies mastered by prekindergarten and kindergarten children

WHO CAN ADMINISTER: Teachers and/or teacher aides who have studied the manual

TIME TO ADMINISTER: 20 to 25 minutes

DESCRIPTION: This criterion-referenced instrument yields a profile of the individual child's strengths and weaknesses in the areas tested and also provides a similar profile for the group tested. The examiner shows pictures to the child, who is asked to describe what is going on in the picture. The child is also instructed to copy geometric shapes and demonstrate coordination by jumping, hopping, and skipping. Areas tested are body part knowledge, color identification, shape identification, number knowledge, story comprehension, multiple directions, large muscle control, auditory memory for meaningful words, visual-motor coordination, sentence recall, vocabulary, visual memory, letter naming, visual-auditory discrimination. The examiner records each child's response in an individual test booklet and completes an 8-item checklist to record the child's behavior during assessment (attention span, body movement, confidence, etc.). A 19-page interpretive manual includes suggestions for uses of test results.

NORMS, RELIABILITY, VALIDITY: Manual provides information

SOURCE: Teachers College Press, 1234 Amsterdam Avenue, New York, New York 10027

APPROXIMATE COST: $19 for Card Easel, Manual, Class Record Sheets, and 50 Pupil Response Sheets

Comprehensive Developmental Scale (Testing Instrument for the Project Memphis Program)

AUTHORS: Alton D. Quick, Thomas L. Little, and A. Anne Campbell

DATE: 1974

PURPOSE: To determine the child's developmental functioning by an assessment of skills in order to help special educators plan early childhood remediation programs

AGE RANGE: Birth through 5 years

WHO CAN ADMINISTER: Diagnosticians, teachers, or parents who have studied the instructions

TIME TO ADMINISTER: Unspecified

DESCRIPTION: This Scale contains 160 items which cover 5 areas of functioning. Under each area 2 to 3 items are placed at 3-month age intervals between birth and 5 years. The areas are Personal-Social Skills, Gross Motor Skills, Fine Motor Skills, Language Skills, and Perceptuo-Cognitive Skills. Pass-fail scores are to be used as a rough estimate of the child's developmental levels. The developmental age for each area can be marked on a profile form on the front page of the Scale along with a line showing chronological age.

In the Project Memphis Program, the Developmental Scale is used as a basis for keeping a continuous record of the child's skill assignments and educational gain. The teacher decides how many times a child must receive a passing score before a skill is considered mastered. Lesson plans are available.

NORMS, RELIABILITY, VALIDITY: Manual does not provide information

SOURCE: Fearon-Pitman Publishers, Inc., 6 Davis Drive, Belmont, California 94002

APPROXIMATE COST: $4 for Manual; $5 for 2 Guides and package of 10 each of the Comprehensive Developmental Scale, Developmental Skill Assignment Record, and Continuous Record for Educational Developmental Gain

Comprehensive Identification Process (CIP)

AUTHOR: R. Reid Zehrbach

DATE: 1975

PURPOSE: To identify children who may need assistance before they enter school

AGE RANGE: 2-6 to 5-6 years

WHO CAN ADMINISTER: Trained paraprofessionals, including volunteers, under the supervision of 1 or 2 professionals in the preschool area. A 3 to 4 hour training session is recommended

TIME TO ADMINISTER: 30 minutes, or about 20 children an hour in the team approach

DESCRIPTION: The CIP involves a station approach with a screening team that typically involves a team leader, 3 to 5 child interviewers, 1 parent interviewer, and 2 hearing and vision screeners, preferably specialists.

The child interviewer administers the fine motor, cognitive-verbal, and gross motor tasks and observes and notes the child's social and emotional development, hearing and vision ability, and general physical development. He/she also may conduct the speech and expressive language screening if thoroughly trained and monitored by a speech clinician.

Tasks assessing the fine motor, cognitive-verbal, and gross motor skills are arranged according to 6 age levels ranging from 30 to 35 months to 60 to 65 months. There are 5 representative tasks typically demonstrated by children at each of these age levels. Instructions are given in the manual for evaluating and interpreting performance on each task in terms of Pass, Rescreen, or Evaluate with a thorough diagnostic work-up.

The Speech and Expressive Language Record Form contains items based on articulation, voice, fluency, and expressive language. Additional items are to be completed by a speech clinician. A 4-page Parent Interview Form includes questions concerning prenatal, personal, medical, developmental, behavioral, and social history. An Observation of Behavior Form contains several items for each of the following areas: hearing and receptive language, vision, physical/motor, speech and expressive language, social behavior, and affective behavior. A Record Folder shows results of hearing and vision screening and summarizes information from the several forms mentioned above. The final recommendation is given in terms of Pass, Rescreen, or Evaluate Further.

NORMS, RELIABILITY, VALIDITY: None reported in the manual

SOURCE: Scholastic Testing Service, Inc., Bensenville, Illinois 60106

APPROXIMATE COST: $60 for Manual, Forms, and materials for 35 Screenings

Dallas Pre-School Screening Test

AUTHORS: Robert R. Percival and Suzanne Poxon
DATE: 1972
PURPOSE: To discover learning disabilities of young children
AGE RANGE: 3 to 6 years
WHO CAN ADMINISTER: Teachers and other professionals who have studied the manual
TIME TO ADMINISTER: 15 minutes
DESCRIPTION: The test screens 6 primary learning areas:

1. Auditory (listening, discrimination, memory)
2. Language (receptive, expressive, communication)
3. Motor (gross and fine motor coordination)
4. Visual (drawings, color discriminations, geometric designs)
5. Psychological (vocabulary and number concepts)
6. Articulation (phonemes, initial and final positions)

Items include questions concerning general information and such tasks as counting, noun association, color naming, matching, and picture description. Developmental age levels are given for each item, ranging from 3 to 6 years, and a Profile Sheet summarizes information. The author emphasizes that additional evaluation should be used when learning disabilities are identified. The manual includes suggestions for writing plans for the individual child's educational development. The test is available in a Spanish edition for biligual administrators.

NORMS, RELIABILITY, VALIDITY: Information available
SOURCE: Dallas Educational Service, P.O. Box 1254, Richardson, Texas 75080
APPROXIMATE COST: $29 for Manual, Cards, 25 Pupil Record Forms and Profile Sheets, and Teacher's and Counselor's Guide

Delco-Elfman Developmental Achievement Test (Clinical And Research Edition)

AUTHOR: Rose M. Elfman
PURPOSE: To evaluate the child's present levels of functioning
AGE RANGE: 6 months to 6 years

WHO CAN ADMINISTER: Teachers and other child specialists who have studied the test manual
TIME TO ADMINISTER: Unspecified
DESCRIPTION: The test consists of 96 items. There are 8 items for each 6-month period from 6 months to 6 years. These items are grouped according to 3 areas; each has 2 or 3 subheadings as indicated below:

1. Physical: Mobility, Visual Motor Coordination
2. Social: Oral Communication, Self-Help, Interpersonal Relationships
3. Intellectual: Information, Cognition, Oral Comprehension/ Memory

Criterion for scoring is included with each item; for example, "*Gestures.* Child uses gestures and other activities to communicate if his oral speech is not comprehended." Testing is discontinued in a category after 4 continuous failures. A Summary Chart that contains all items in brief form allows a profile to be drawn according to area of function and age. Instructions are given in the manual for calculating category Age Achievement Scores and a Developmental Achievement Test Age from the total score. The manual contains test pictures and a list of materials that are to be assembled by the examiner.
NORMS, RELIABILITY, VALIDITY: None reported in manual
SOURCE: Rose Marks Elfman, Delaware County Intermediate Unit, 6th and Olive Streets, Media, Pennsylvania 19063
APPROXIMATE COST: $6 for Manual and 24 Answer Sheets

Denver Developmental Screening Test (DDST)

AUTHORS: William K. Frankenburg and Josiah B. Dodds
DATE: 1969
PURPOSE: To detect significant motor, social, and/or language delays through use of a series of developmental tasks and milestones
AGE RANGE: 1 month to 6 years
WHO CAN ADMINISTER: Clinicians, specialists, teachers, nurses, paraprofessionals, and volunteers who have reached proficiency designated in the DDST Training Package
TIME TO ADMINISTER: 10 to 20 minutes

DESCRIPTION: The DDST consists of 105 items that are grouped according to the sectors of Personal-Social (**Ex:** "Puts on clothing"); Fine Motor-Adaptive (**Ex:** "Draws a man with 3 parts"); Language (**Ex:** "Combines two different words"); and Gross Motor (**Ex:** "Sits without support"). On the 1-page test form, an age range of expected performance is shown for each of the items. Initially only tasks pertaining to the child's age (approximately 20 items) are administered. These are scored on the form as Pass, Fail, or Questionable and give a profile of the child's performance. Final results for each sector are categorized as "normal," "abnormal," or "questionable." The reference manual gives detailed instructions for administration, scoring, interpretation, etc. During administration of the DDST, the mother is present when possible and some items are based on her report, but direct observation by the examiner should be used whenever possible. Instructional materials, including films, are available for training administrators in order that the test will be used properly. The test was developed at the University of Colorado Medical Center. The manual is available in Spanish.

NORMS, RELIABILITY, VALIDITY: Manual provides detailed information

SOURCE: The LADOCA Project and Publishing Foundation, Inc., East 51st Avenue and Lincoln Street, Denver, Colorado 80216

APPROXIMATE COST: $9 for Test Kit, Rererence Manual, and 25 Test Forms

Denver Prescreening Developmental Questionnaire (PDQ)

AUTHORS: William K. Frankenburg, William J. van Doorninck, Theresa N. Liddell, and Nathan P. Dick

DATE: 1975

PURPOSE: To identify children who should be more thoroughly screened with the Denver Developmental Screening Test (DDST) and to serve as an ongoing log of the child's developmental program

AGE RANGE: 3 months to 6 years

WHO CAN ADMINISTER: Parent completes questionnaire after being instructed by an assistant or aide

TIME TO ADMINISTER: 2 to 5 minutes

DESCRIPTION: The questionnaire can be completed by a parent in such settings as day-care centers, public-health clinics, and private physicians' offices. The PDQ consists of 97 items in order of developmental difficulty from ages 3 months to 6 years. An assistant calculates the child's age and shows the parent a group of 10 consecutive questions that are to be answered. The assistant also helps the parent if necessary. An example, at the 2 year 3 month level, is "Does your child feed himself with a spoon or fork without spilling much?" The parent answers "Yes," "No," "Child refuses to try," or "Child has not had the chance to try." The assistant follows specific instructions for scoring and determines from the instruction sheets what recommendations are to be made. For example, if there are only 6 "Yes" responses, the child should be evaluated further with the Denver Developmental Screening Instrument on which the PDQ is based. The PDQ was developed at the University of Colorado Medical Center. Material is available in French and Spanish.

NORMS, RELIABILITY, VALIDITY: Information available

SOURCE: The LADOCA Project and Publishing Foundation, Inc., East 51st Avenue and Lincoln Street, Denver, Colorado 80216

APPROXIMATE COST: $4 for each of 5 pads of 100 Questionnaires (each pad covers a specific age range)

Developmental Activities Screening Inventory (DASI)

AUTHORS: Rebecca F. Du Bose and Mary Beth Langley

DATE: 1977

PURPOSE: To provide early detection of developmental disabilities

AGE RANGE: 6 months to 5 years

WHO CAN ADMINISTER: Teachers who have studied the manual, clinicians, or specialists

TIME TO ADMINISTER: 25 minutes

DESCRIPTION: The DASI is a nonverbal informal screening measure consisting of 55 test items, which assess a variety of developmental skills. These include fine-motor manipulation, knowledge of cause-effect and means-end relationships, associations, number concepts, size discriminations, and sequencing. Tasks are listed by 6-month age levels beginning with 6 to 11 months, and ending with 54 to 60 months. There are 6 items for each age level (**Ex:** At the 36 to 41 month level one item is "Demonstrates understanding of concepts of *two* and *three*"). Adaptations may be made for children with visual, auditory, or other impairments. Specific instructions are given for establishing a basal and ceiling level in order that all items do not have to be administered to each child. Scores are translated to a Developmental Quotient. The 46-page manual suggests examples of simple instructional programs from analysis of failed items.

NORMS, RELIABILITY, VALIDITY: Information available

SOURCE: Teaching Resources Corporation, 100 Bolyston Street, Boston, Massachusetts 02116

APPROXIMATE COST: $65 for Manual, 50 Student Response Forms, and manipulative materials

Developmental Indicators for the Assessment of Learning (DIAL)

AUTHORS: Carol Mardell and Dorothea Goldenberg

DATE: 1973

PURPOSE: To identify children in need of follow-up services because of learning problems

AGE RANGE: 2-6 yo 5-6 years

WHO CAN ADMINISTER: Requires 4 examiners who function as a team; examiners can be teachers, parent volunteers or paraprofessionals who are trained in about 2 hours to administer DIAL. The coordinator or team leader should be a professional in special education, early childhood, psychology, speech and language, or other related fields.

TIME TO ADMINISTER: 20 to 30 minutes per child (6 to 8 children per hour)

DESCRIPTION: DIAL is a multidimension screening test that requires a station approach. Four stations are set up to screen for the following areas of functioning:

1. Gross Motor (throwing, catching, jumping, hopping, skipping, standing still, balancing)
2. Fine Motor (matching, building, cutting, copying shapes,

copying letters, touching fingers, clapping hands)
3. Concept (sorting blocks and classifying, naming colors, counting, identifying body parts)
4. Communications (articulating, remembering, naming nouns and verbs, coping, naming self, age, and sex, classifying foods, telling a story)

The examiner at each station also notes his/her subjective impression of 12 behaviors. Examples of these are: "squints/rubs eyes," is "disruptive," is "lethargic," is "impulsive."

The manual gives instructions for administration, which include description of physical facilities, floor plan, orientation toward child, and specific responsibilities for each person on the team (the coordinator, 4 examiners, and 3 optional volunteers). The coordinator receives the completed scoresheets and makes decisions about the follow-up (retesting, referral, etc.) based on the child's performance at each station. Interpretations and decisions are partly based on how many, if any, areas of functioning fall below suggested cut-off points. Training materials are available and training workshops may be arranged. Cards, which may be distributed to parents, contain suggested enrichment or remedial experiences that parents may provide at home for each area of functioning.

NORMS, RELIABILITY, VALIDITY: Manual provides detailed information

SOURCE: DIAL, Inc., Box 911, Highland Park, Illinois 60035

APPROXIMATE COST: $125 for Dial Assessment Kit; $13 for set of 50 Parent Cards

Developmental Profile

AUTHORS: Gerald D. Alpern and Thomas J. Boll
DATE: 1972
PURPOSE: To assess children's development multidimensionally without sexual or racial bias, to aid in parent counseling, and to provide an individual curriculum guide for normal and retarded children.
AGE RANGE: Birth to preadolescence (for normal children, birth to about 9 years; for handicapped, any age where skills are not expected to extend beyond the 11 to 12 year ceiling)

WHO CAN ADMINISTER: Teachers, teachers' aides, physicians, social workers, medical aides, and psychologists (by studying the manual if trained in testing or interviewing; others may require brief instructions and supervision by a professional capable of self-instruction)

TIME TO ADMINISTER: 30 to 40 minutes

DESCRIPTION: This instrument is designed to be used as a structured interview technique, with the parent answering questions about the child, but can also be used by the teacher to evaluate children directly. A total of 217 items are arranged into 5 scales (physical, self-help, social, academic, and communication). For example, an item on the Physical Scale at the 13 to 18 months level is, "Has the child stopped drooling?" (This item is passed if "No drooling occurs except during chewing when eating."). Each scale proceeds in 6-month intervals from birth to 3-6 years and thereafter by 1-year intervals; each interval contains 3 items. Any or all 5 scales may be used. When all 5 scales are used, the resulting profile identifies the age level at which the child is functioning in each area. The wire-bound manual contains, in addition to the tab-indexed inventory, 70 pages of test description, instructions, tables, and discussion of statistics.

NORMS, RELIABILITY, VALIDITY: Manual provides detailed information

SOURCE: Psychological Development Publications, 7150 Lakeside Drive, Indianapolis, Indiana 46278

APPROXIMATE COST: $10 for Interviewing Set Manual and 10 Profile and Scoring Forms

Early Childhood Inventories Project

AUTHORS: Alan Coller and Jack Victor

DATE: 1970

PURPOSE: To evaluate a child's abilities in several developmental areas

AGE RANGE: Prekindergarten and kindergarten

WHO CAN ADMINISTER: Teachers who have studied the manual and paraprofessionals who have been trained to administer the instrument

Time to Administer: Unspecified

Description: These Inventories constitute a series of experimental instruments developed at the Institute for Developmental Studies, School of Education, New York University. The Inventories are listed below under six areas:

1. General Identification
   Body Parts Inventory
   Color Name Inventory
   Shape Name Inventory
   Classroom Objects Vocabulary Inventory
2. Pre-Mathematics and Mathematics
   Relational Concepts Inventory/Pre-Mathematics
   Quantity Matching Inventory/Mathematics
   Set Matching Inventory/Mathematics
   Numeral Name Inventory
3. Pre-Science and Science
   Relational Concepts Inventory/Pre-Science
4. General Concepts
   Same/Different Inventory 1 and 3 (2 not available)
5. Reading, Spelling and Articulation
   Alphabet Name Inventory/Printed Upper Case
   Alphabet Name Inventory/Printed Lower Case
6. Linguistic Concepts
   Comparatives Inventory/Linguistic Concept
   Prepositions Inventory/Linguistic Concept

Each Inventory with accompanying instructions and testing material is in mimeographed form. A 14-page descriptive summary of all Inventories is available.

Norms, Reliability, Validity: Information available for some of the Inventories

Source: Alan R. Coller, Research for Better Schools, Inc., Suite 1700, 1700 Market Street, Philadelphia, Pennsylvania 19103

Approximate Cost: Available from above source

Hawaii Early Learning Profile (HELP)

Authors: Developed by the School of Public Health at the University of Hawaii
Date: 1979

PURPOSE: To evaluate developmental skills in small incremental steps in order to determine needs and objectives

AGE RANGE: Birth to 36 months

WHO CAN ADMINISTER: Parents, teachers, and other professionals who have studied the charts and activity guide

TIME TO ADMINISTER: Unspecified

DESCRIPTION: This instrument consists of over 650 developmentally sequenced skills listed by approximate age levels on 3 horizontal charts. The items were developed from a wide range of tests and assessment programs. Vertical lines on the charts indicate each month from birth to 3 years. The 3 large charts (11 by 28 inch) are also divided into 6 areas: Cognitive/Intellectual, Expressive Language, Gross Motor, Fine Motor, Socio-Emotional, and Self-Help. Each item is numbered to facilitate reference to an Activity Guide, which describes the item more fully and suggests activities that may be used to help the child accomplish the skill. For example, an item at the 11- to 13-month level is "Stands a few seconds," with the criterion "Place the child in a standing position. Remove your support. The child should remain standing two to three seconds." Five activities are then described that might be used to help the child learn the skill. According to the test developers, the suggested training acitvities are considered to be particularly helpful for handicapped children. The Activity Guide also discusses additional uses of the developmental materials.

NORMS, RELIABILITY, VALIDITY: None reported in Activity Guide

SOURCE: VORT Corporation, Box 11757 N, Palo Alto, California 94306

APPROXIMATE COST: $40 for Activity Guide and 10 sets of Charts

Individual Learning Disabilities Classroom Screening Instrument: Preschool/Kindergarten Level (ILDCSI-P/K)

AUTHORS: Marian T. Giles in cooperation with Angeline M. Jacobs, Penny Spector, and Donna Stefferud

DATE: 1973

PURPOSE: To provide preliminary and very early identification of children with possible learning and/or emotional problems

AGE RANGE: Preschool-Kindergarten

WHO CAN ADMINISTER: Teachers who have familiarized themselves with the behavioral items and observed the child in the normal course of the day's activities

TIME TO ADMINISTER: Unspecified (checklist)

DESCRIPTION: The test booklet contains 36 items that the teacher checks according to a scale of Unobserved, Average, Moderate, or Severe. Twenty-nine items are based on observation. Examples of these are: "confuses left and right directionality"; "is unable to walk the length of a four-inch wide balance beam without stepping off"; "is afraid of many things most peers do not fear." Seven items require direct testing with the child:

1. Visual-Memory (**Ex:** Placing colored crayons in the same order as shown)
2. Visual-Motor Integration (**Ex:** Copying geometric forms)
3. Auditory Memory (**Ex:** Repeating phrases)
4. Visual Closure (**Ex:** Recognizing what is missing in a picture)
5. Discrimination of Tones (**Ex:** Discriminating tones, from xylophone or sound blocks, as being higher or lower)
6. Visual Figure-ground (**Ex:** Pointing to a specified object hidden in a picture)
7. Motor-Crossing Midline (**Ex:** Copying teacher's movements involving crossing midline with one arm)

The last page of the test booklet contains a form for recording birth, developmental, medical, social, and preschool data.

The 35-page manual gives specific instructions for scoring, and scores are translated in such a way that a profile shows problems in the areas of visual, auditory, verbal, social-emotional, and integration. Recommendations are made for interpretation with regard to the need for various types of intervention. The manual includes a discussion of remedial and preventive techniques for the several areas of disabilities with a bibliography for each area.

NORMS, RELIABILITY, VALIDITY: Information available

SOURCE: Learning Pathways, Inc., Box 1407, Evergreen, Colorado 80439

APPROXIMATE COST: $16 for Manual, 10 Classroom Screening Instruments, and Scoring Masks

Kindergarten Screening Inventory

AUTHORS: Developed by the Houston Independent School District

DATE: 1975

PURPOSE: To screen for possible difficulties that could lead to learning problems

AGE RANGE: Beginning kindergarten

WHO CAN ADMINISTER: A team of volunteers who relate well to children and who have had several hours of training by professionals in several areas

TIME TO ADMINISTER: 30 minutes per child (4 to 10 minutes for each station)

DESCRIPTION: The screening involves a team of examiners using a station approach. The child's native language is to be used during testing. Areas screened are:

1. Distant Vision (**Ex:** Child points to letters on a small card as each letter is pointed to on a wall chart by an examiner.)
2. Hearing (**Ex:** Child listens to three words on a tape recording and identifies corresponding pictures as they are named.)
3. Eye-Hand Coordination (**Ex:** Child copies geometric designs, draws a picture of a boy or girl, completes a circular maze, etc.)
4. Language-Learning (**Ex:** Child gives age, name, identifies body parts, counts, repeats digits, etc.)
5. Gross Motor (**Ex:** Child skips, hops, jumps, throws a bean bag, etc.)

Instructions are given in the manual for administering items and scoring in terms of Adequate, Referred, or No Response. The child's percentile rank for each area can be determined from appropriate tables. In addition to the station screening procedures, separate rating scales (checklists) for each area are to be completed by the child's classroom teacher. A manual of follow-up remedial and training activities is available.

NORMS, RELIABILITY, VALIDITY: Information provided in Technical Manual

SOURCE: Houston Independent School District, 3830 Richmond Avenue, Houston, Texas 77027

APPROXIMATE COST: Available from above source

The K-Q: Kindergarten Questionnaire

AUTHORS: Susan Berger and Evelyn Perlman
DATE: 1976
PURPOSE: To detect emotional, learning, speech, health, and perceptual problems at the prekindergarten level and to facilitate intervention where indicated
AGE RANGE: 4 to 6 years (children entering kindergarten)
WHO CAN ADMINISTER: Teachers and/or members of a pupil personnel department who have attended a workshop on administration of this instrument
TIME TO ADMINISTER: 20 to 30 minutes
DESCRIPTION: This screening instrument was designed to involve all members of the pupil personnel department and the parents of each child being tested. Responsibilities of each individual are listed in the manual in a checklist form, as well as a suggested sequence for each step of the screening procedure. The interviewer administers the Child's Form portion of the test in the presence of the parent. This portion requires the child to draw a man, copy geometric shapes, demonstrate gross motor skills, etc. Meanwhile the parent completes a 4-page duplicated questionnaire that elicits information about the child's family, health, emotional and social development, motor development, handedness, school readiness behaviors, and previous school experience. Information from the Parent Form and the Child's Form is transferred to an individual data card for each child. A K-Q follow-up manual is provided to help interpret test results.
NORMS, RELIABILITY, VALIDITY: Manual provides information
SOURCE: Evelyn Perlman, 10 Tyler Road, Lexington, Massachusetts 02173
APPROXIMATE COST: $13 for Manual, 25 Parent Questionnaires, 25 Child Questionnaires, and 25 Individual Data Cards

Koontz Child Developmental Program: Training Activities for the First 48 Months

AUTHOR: Charles W. Koontz

DATE: 1974
PURPOSE: To evaluate and improve the development of normal children and the retarded who are functioning at developmental levels of 1 to 48 months
AGE RANGE: 1 to 48 months
WHO CAN ADMINISTER: Parents, teachers, pediatricians, therapists, and psychologists who have studied the manual and who have observed the child for at least 1 week before attempting evaluation
TIME TO ADMINISTER: Unspecified
DESCRIPTION: Four functional areas of development are considered: Gross Motor, Fine Motor, Social, and Language. There are 25 performance items at each of 22 age levels. Operational definitions are included for each item. For example, "Walks short distance" is defined as "ability to walk unassisted 10 feet in a normal manner with equidistant alternation of feet." The administrator starts at one level above the level at which the child can already perform all items. A profile is obtained that is then compared with the child's chronological age to note items or areas of development that need improvement or training. The performance items and training activities comprise a large portion of the manual. Training activities and suggestions are shown on the page opposite the item itself. The author emphasizes that age levels are approximate and that the program was not designed to require the child to perform items on command but should represent the typical behavior.
NORMS, RELIABILITY, VALIDITY: Manual provides information
SOURCE: Western Psychological Services, 12031 Wilshire Boulevard, Los Angeles, California 90025
APPROXIMATE COST: $15 for the Manual and 25 Record Cards

Learning Accomplishment Profile (LAP)

AUTHOR: Anne R. Sanford
DATE: 1974
PURPOSE: To observe the child's developmental level in order to set up learning objectives
AGE RANGE: 1 month to 6 years
WHO CAN ADMINISTER: Teachers and others who have been

trained to administer the instrument

TIME TO ADMINISTER: Unspecified (checklist)

DESCRIPTION: The LAP lists approximately 500 developmental items that are compiled from 15 sources of developmental materials. The items are grouped by age levels between 1 month and 6 years and are divided into 6 areas:

1. Gross Motor (**Ex:** "Jumps from bottom step")
2. Fine Motor Skills (**Ex:** "Copies a circle")
3. Social Skills (**Ex:** "Understands sharing")
4. Self-Help Skills (**Ex:** "Unbuttons accessible buttons")
5. Cognitive Skills (**Ex:** "Counts two blocks")
6. Language Skills (**Ex:** "Names own drawing")

The tasks are scored Pass or Fail according to the teacher's general knowledge of the child's typical behavior or from observation of planned activities. The 121-page manual gives detailed instructions for scoring. The child's developmental age for each area of functioning is considered to be at the level immediately preceding the one at which the child is unable to accomplish four of five consecutive tasks. Failed items then become objectives that provide guidance in sequencing skill development. A profile can be charted to show initial developmental age and subsequent progress. Teaching suggestions are given in the profile booklet and additional teaching materials are available.

An amplified LAP for infants (newborn to approximately 33 months) is also available

NORMS, RELIABILITY, VALIDITY: None reported in manual

SOURCE: Kaplan School Supply Corporation, 600 Jonestown Road, Winston-Salem, North Carolina 27103

APPROXIMATE COST: $3 for the Manual and $3 for each Learning Accomplishment Profile Booklet

Lexington Developmental Scale and Lexington Developmental Scale Screening Instrument

AUTHOR: John V. Irwin

DATE: 1977

PURPOSE: To portray graphically the child's developmental level and to identify training objectives

AGE RANGE: Birth to 6 years

WHO CAN ADMINISTER: Teachers, nurses, and social workers who have studied the manual; others who have been trained to administer the instrument

TIME TO ADMINISTER: Long Form, 60 to 90 minutes; Short Form, 30 to 45 minutes

DESCRIPTION: The Developmental Scale consists of 414 items and the Screening Instrument consists of 207 items. These are arranged by 4 areas of functioning. Items for each area are listed according to 1-year age levels ranging from 2 years to 6 years. An infant scale lists items at half-year levels from birth to 2 years. The scale evaluates the following areas (examples are given at the 3 to 4 year level):

1. Motor (**Ex:** "Walks up and down stairs alternating feet without support")
2. Language (**Ex:** "Names 20 or more pictures of common objects")
3. personal and Social (**Ex:** "Understands sharing")
4. Cognitive (**Ex:** "When do you eat breakfast?")

There is a separate 1-page chart for each area. After items are checked on the appropriate chart, a profile may be drawn. In addition, an 18-item Emotional Scale is completed. Results indicate whether there is need for further testing or referral to specialists in different areas. The charts may also be used as a basis for planning both individual and group activities. Teaching suggestions are available.

NORMS, RELIABILITY, VALIDITY: Manual provides information

SOURCE: United Cerebral Palsy of the Bluegrass, Inc., P. O. Box 8003, Lexington, Kentucky 40503

APPROXIMATE COST: $4 for Administrator's Manual and 10 Short-Form Charts

Marshalltown Behavioral Developmental Profile — Standardized Revision (MBDP-SR)

AUTHORS: Revision and standardization by Robert W. Fuqua, Gary D. Phye, and Mel Walden.

DATE: 1979

PURPOSE: To identify handicapped children and determine

their particular developmental strengths and weaknesses in order to plan specific instructional intervention
AGE RANGE: Birth to 6 years
WHO CAN ADMINISTER: Teachers who have studied the manual
TIME TO ADMINISTER: 45 to 60 minutes
DESCRIPTION: The MBDP-SR consists of a motor, a cognitive, and a socialization scale, with 72 items per scale. On each scale there are 6 items at each of twelve 6-month age levels. The following examples of scale items are from the 19 to 24 months level:

1. Motor Scale (**Ex:** "Correctly nests 4 or more nesting cups")
2. Cognitive Scale (**Ex:** "Selects item from group of five items")
3. Socialization Scale (**Ex:** "Verbalizes toilet needs")

Each item is immediately followed by instructions for administering and the criterion for passing that particular item. Each of the scales yields a Developmental Quotient; the three scales together produce a Full Scale Developmental Quotient. The test kit includes most of the materials needed for administering the instrument. The manual contains a list of common materials which are to be collected by the test administrator. The 24-page manual and the three scales are contained in a loose-leaf binder.
NORMS, RELIABILITY, VALIDITY: Manual provides information
SOURCE: Marshalltown Project, Preschool Division, A.E.A. 6, 507 East Anson Street, Marshalltown, Iowa 50158
APPROXIMATE COST: $80 for Manual, 30 Scoring and Report Forms, and Test Kit

McCarthy Screening Test (MST)

AUTHOR: Dorothea McCarthy
DATE: 1978
PURPOSE: To identify children who are likely to need special educational assistance
AGE RANGE: 4-0 to 6-5 years
WHO CAN ADMINISTER: Teachers and paraprofessionals who have been thoroughly instructed in its use by experienced ad-

ministrators of the McCarthy Scale of Children's Abilities (MSCA) and who have had supervised practice

TIME TO ADMINISTER: 20 minutes

DESCRIPTION: The MST consists of 6 tests of the McCarthy Scales of Children's Abilities, which were selected as representative of the MSCA. These tests are:

1. Right-Left Orientation (**Ex:** Child identifies left and right body parts, etc.)
2. Verbal Memory (**Ex:** Child repeats words and sentences)
3. Draw-A-Design (**Ex:** Child copies geometric designs)
4. Numerical Memory (**Ex:** Child repeats sequences of digits)
5. Conceptual Grouping (**Ex:** Child classifies blocks of different shapes, sizes, and colors)
6. Leg Coordination (**Ex:** Child stands on one foot, tiptoes, etc.)

The 65-page manual gives instructions for determining the risk classification based on transferring raw scores to percentiles for chronological age and recommends that "at risk" children undergo further assessment.

NORMS, RELIABILITY, VALIDITY: Manual provides detailed information and reference is made to the MSCA for additional technical information

SOURCE: The Psychological Corporation, 757 Third Avenue, New York, New York 10017

APPROXIMATE COST: $28 for Manual, 25 Record Forms, 25 Drawing Booklets, and necessary testing materials

The Meeting Street School Screening Test: Early Identification of Children with Learning Disabilities

AUTHORS: Peter K. Hainsworth and Marian L. Siqueland

DATE: 1969

PURPOSE: To survey gross motor, visual-perceptual-motor, and language skills in order to provide early identification of children with learning disabilities and to initiate modification of their school program

AGE RANGE: 5-0 to 7-5 years

WHO CAN ADMINISTER: Teachers and lay personnel who are

trained to administer the test through observation of an experienced examiner followed by careful study of the manual and supervised practice on a few children

TIME TO ADMINISTER: 15 to 20 minutes

DESCRIPTION: In the 126-page manual the authors discuss general aspects of learning disabilities based on an information processing model. Three types of testing are used:

1. The *Motor Patterning* subtest consists of items classified according to Gait Patterns, Clap Hands, Hand Patterns, Follow Directions I (assesses child's ability to comprehend and retain verbal directions such as "Take two steps forward and one step backward"), and Touch Fingers.
2. The *Visual-Perceptual-Motor* subtest involves Block Tapping, Visual Matching, Visual Memory, Copy Forms, and Follow Directions II (samples child's understanding of spatial and directional concepts with such directions as "Draw a ball behind the car").
3. The *Language* subtest consists of Repeat Words, Repeat Sentences, Counting, Tell a Story (from a picture), and Language Sequencing (child supplies the last word in a sequence of three words such as "Breakfast, lunch, and ———").

During testing the examiner observes and rates the child's behavior on such aspects as attention, orientation, and self-correction. The manual gives instructions for converting raw scores to a profile based on each subtest by age. Cut-off points on the raw score are used to estimate which children are high risk for learning disabilities.

NORMS, RELIABILITY, VALIDITY: Manual provides detailed information

SOURCE: Meeting Street School, 667 Waterman Avenue, East Providence, Rhode Island 02914

APPROXIMATE COST: $17 for Manual and 50 Screening Tests

Minnesota Child Development Inventory

AUTHORS: Harold Ireton and Edward Thwing
DATE: 1974

PURPOSE: To provide a systematic means of obtaining and summarizing the mother's observations of her child

AGE RANGE: 1 to 6 years

WHO CAN ADMINISTER: Questionnaire is completed by mother who is aware of the child's behavior and who can read at an eighth grade level or above

TIME TO ADMINISTER: Unspecified (questionnaire)

DESCRIPTION: The Inventory consists of 320 short statements about behaviors of children, which the mother marks Yes or No. She shows responses by filling in a circle on a score sheet, which is separate from the test booklet. Items are in random order but the manual includes a listing of the items by developmental sequence and by area assessed. These areas follow: Gross Motor (**Ex:** "Skips"), Fine Motor (**Ex:** "Claps hands"), Expressive Language (**Ex:** "Talks on the telephone"), Comprehensive-Conceptual (**Ex:** "Counts to ten"), Situation Comprehension (**Ex:** "Opens door by turning knob"), Self-Help (**Ex:** "Ties shoelaces"), Personal-Social (**Ex:** "Actively refuses to obey"), and General Development, which is a summary scale. Complete instructions are given in the manual for scoring, which may be done by hand or by machine, and for preparing a profile by sex according to the several areas. Cut-off points for interpretation (to be done by a clinician) are suggested and discussed. The authors stress that results are to be interpreted to indicate development *below* expectation for age rather than normal or accelerated development.

NORMS, RELIABILITY, VALIDITY: Manual provides detailed information

SOURCE: Interpretive Scoring Systems, 4401 West 76th Street Minneapolis, Minnesota 55435

APPROXIMATE COST: $33 for Manual, 10 Inventory Booklets, 100 Answer Sheets, 50 Male and 50 Female Profile Forms, and Scoring Templates

Observational Checklist

AUTHORS: Alice H. Hayden, Robert K. Smith, Karen von Hippel, and Sandra A. Baer

DATE: 1978
PURPOSE: To call attention to behaviors that require more careful observation and ongoing assessment
AGE RANGE: 3 to 6 years
WHO CAN ADMINISTER: Teachers who have observed children in their program
TIME TO ADMINISTER: Unspecified (checklist)
DESCRIPTION: This checklist contains 42 items grouped under 5 areas: Communicative Skills, Motor Skills, Social Skills, Vision or Hearing Skills, and General Health. For each item (**Ex:** "Does the child seem to have difficulty following directions?") the teacher checks Yes, No, or Sometimes. The checklist, instructions for scoring, and interpretations are included in the 131-page publication listed below. There is also an annotated bibliography of books about learning disabilities.
NORMS, RELIABILITY, VALIDITY: None reported in publication
SOURCE: *Mainstreaming Preschoolers: Children with Learning Disabilities.* Superintendent of Documents, U. S. Government Printing Office, Washington, D. C. 20402
APPROXIMATE COST: $4 for book

Observational Developmental Assessment for Preschools: The Brekken Drouin Developmental Spotcheck

AUTHORS: Linda Brekken and Chris Drouin
DATE: 1978
PURPOSE: To determine areas of developmental strengths and weaknesses
AGE RANGE: 2 to 6 years
WHO CAN ADMINSTER: Consultants, administrators, or teachers who have studied the manual and have observed children in the school setting; paraprofessionals and parents if training has been provided
TIME TO ADMINISTER: Unspecified (checklist)
DESCRIPTION: The instrument consists of 16 items for each of 5 scales. There are 2 items for each 6-month interval between 24 and 60 months and 4 items for the 12-month interval between 60 and 72 months. The 5 scales are Gross Motor, Perceptual Motor, Fine Motor, Language, and Social and Self-Help. Each

item includes a definition to be used in scoring. For example, the definition for "Skips on one foot" is "Skips on one foot; skips with one foot only; sometimes called 'galloping.' " The child is to be observed in a natural classroom setting, but the examiner may need to find situations in which the child demonstrates the behavior. In order to fill this need, the authors include suggestions for classroom activities. A profile that shows strengths and weaknesses may be drawn according to area of functioning and age level.

NORMS, RELIABILITY, VALIDITY: None reported in manual

SOURCE: Linda Brekken, Casa Colina Hospital, Children's Developmental Services, 255 East Bonita Avenue, Pomona, California 91767

APPROXIMATE COST: $5 for instructions, research paper, and forms ($15 with corresponding curriculum)

Parent Readiness Evaluation of Preschoolers (PREP)

AUTHOR: A. Edward Ahr

DATE: 1968

PURPOSE: To allow parents to gain objective information about their child to supplement their subjective opinions

AGE RANGE: 3-9 to 5-8 years

WHO CAN ADMINISTER: Parents who have studied the manual

TIME TO ADMINISTER: One hour (may be administered in two sessions)

DESCRIPTION: The test is made up of two sections, Verbal and Performance. In the Verbal section the child responds verbally to the parent's questions or statements. There are 89 items in this section, 4 to 15 items in each of 8 subtests:

1. General Information (**Ex:** Child answers questions about days of the week, seasons, animals, etc.)
2. Comprehension (**Ex:** Child responds "yes" or "no" to questions such as "Do stoves heat?")
3. Opposites (**Ex:** Child gives opposite of word stated by parent)
4. Identification (**Ex:** Parent places 10 common objects in a sock and asks the child to identify each object through touch)

5. Verbal Associations (**Ex:** Child answers questions such as "What would you use to open a *lock?*")
6. Verbal Description (**Ex:** Parent shows child an object such as a banana and asks the child to tell all about it)
7. Listening (**Ex:** Parent says two to six words in succession and asks the child to repeat them)
8. Language (**Ex:** Parent points to picture in test booklet and asks child to complete a statement such as, "Here is a foot, here are two ———.")

The Performance section consists of 58 items in 5 subtests and requires the child to point to or mark pictures in the test booklet. The subtests are:

1. Concepts (**Ex:** Child marks pictures of items named by parent)
2. Motor Coordination (**Ex:** Child copies geometric shapes, numerals, and letters, etc.)
3. Visual-Motor Association (**Ex:** Child marks one of four objects that "goes with" the picture at the top of the page)
4. Visual Interpretation (**Ex:** Child marks one of four objects that is "something like" the picture at the top of the page)
5. Memory (**Ex:** Parent says two to three words in succession, waits 20 seconds, and then shows child several pictures and asks the child to mark pictures of the words he/she just said)

The 25-page test manual includes instructions for administering and scoring the test. A table in the manual helps the parent determine whether the child's performance on the PREP test was above average, average, or below average.

NORMS, RELIABLITY, VALIDITY: Manual provides information
SOURCE: Priority Innovations Inc., P. O. Box 792, Skokie, Illinois 60076
APPROXIMATE COST: $25 for 10 Parents' Test Manuals and 10 Child's Test Booklets

Portage Guide to Early Education: Checklist

AUTHORS: Susan Bluma, Marsha Shearer, Alma Frohman, and Jean Hilliard

DATE: 1976

PURPOSE: To evaluate a child's developmental level, either handicapped or normal, in order to plan an educational program

AGE RANGE: Birth to 6 years

WHO CAN ADMINISTER: Teachers and paraprofessionals who have had training in the Portage Project

TIME TO ADMINISTER: 20 to 40 minutes

DESCRIPTION: The behavioral checklist consists of a 25-page booklet, which contains 580 developmentally sequenced behaviors. The first 45 items are grouped under "Infant Stimulation" (**Ex:** "Follows light with eyes"). Other sections assess the following areas (with examples at the 4 and 5 year level):

1. Socialization (**Ex:** "Contributes to adult conversation")
2. Language (**Ex:** "Carries out a series of 3 directions")
3. Self-Help (**Ex:** "Washes hands and face")
4. Cognitive (**Ex:** "Names eight colors")

For each of the 580 items, there are curriculum cards that provide teaching suggestions. These cards are contained in a card file and are color coded to match corresponding sections in the checklist. When the cards and other teaching guides are used as a home-based program, the teacher essentially helps the mother learn how to teach her own child.

NORMS, RELIABILITY, VALIDITY: Information available

SOURCE: Cooperative Educational Service Agency No. 12, Portage Project, 412 East Slifer Street, Portage, Wisconsin 53901

APPROXIMATE COST: $32 for Manual, 15 Checklist Booklets, and one set of Curriculum Cards

Pre-Academic Learning Inventory (PAL)

AUTHORS: Mildred H. Woods and Fay M. Layne

DATE: 1975

PURPOSE: To provide both quantitative and qualititive data regarding a child's special needs, strengths, weaknesses, and behavior, in order that appropriate education, remediation, parental counseling, or referrals can be initiated

AGE RANGE: Kindergarten to first grade

WHO CAN ADMINISTER: School personnel following 1 to 2 hours of instruction by school psychologist

TIME TO ADMINISTER: 30 to 35 minutes

DESCRIPTION: PAL assesses performance in 9 areas of development considered by the authors to be necessary for academic success. The test also collects information about *how* a child performs each task. These nine skill areas are:

1. Language Development (**Ex:** Examiner records verbatim child's responses to questions, pictures followed by questions, and volunteered language during assessment)
2. Speech Development (**Ex:** Examiner says a word and asks child to repeat it)
3. Concept Development (**Ex:** Examiner asks child to identify colors, count by rote, count pennies, etc.)
4. Body Concept (**Ex:** Child draws a picture of a man)
5. Auditory Channel Development (**Ex:** Examiner says a series of numbers and child repeats them; examiner says a word and child selects the correct picture from the 3 stimulus pictures)
6. Visual Channel Development (**Ex:** Examiner shows child a series of pictures on a card and child is instructed to make a row of the same pictures in the same order; examiner shows child a design and asks child to find another one just like it)
7. Visual-Motor Integration (**Ex:** Child draws a line between two lines, cuts out a picture with scissors, and throws, catches and bounces a ball)
9. Gross Motor Coordination (**Ex:** Child balances on one foot, hops, and skips)

The 37-page manual gives detailed information on administering, scoring, and interpreting the test.

The 12-page test booklet provides space for recording exact responses on each item as well as the total score for each subtest. Also provided on the test booklet is a page for recording behavioral observations of the child during testing (extremely shy, short attention span, very aggressive, etc.). A profile for each child indicates whether the child is immature, weak, average, strong, or mature in each of the 9 areas.

A Class Record Sheet is available, as well as a Parent-Child

Activities leaflet. After testing, the teacher confers with the parent and then checks the skill areas in the activity leaflet in which the child needs additional developmental experiences.
NORMS, RELIABILITY, VALIDITY: Manual provides information
SOURCE: Educational Dimensions, Ltd., P. O. Box 366, Cedar Falls, Iowa 50613
APPROXIMATE COST: $13 for Manual, Stimulus Pictures, Visual Memory Cards, 25 Record Booklets, 1 Class Record Sheet

Pre-School Attainment Record (PAR) — Research Edition

AUTHOR: Edgar A. Doll
DATE: 1966
PURPOSE: To assess children with or without various types of-handicaps
AGE RANGE: 6 months to 7 years
WHO CAN ADMINISTER: Clinicians or specialists, teachers who have attended a workshop or studied the test manual, and para-professionals who have been trained to conduct the interview (clinicians, school psychologists, or other testing specialists should interpret results)
TIME TO ADMINISTER: 20 to 30 minutes
DESCRIPTION: In this instrument, information is obtained from the mother primarily through a structured interview; some items of information may be obtained through direct observation of the child. The interviewer's goal is to ascertain the child's typical or ordinary behavior. Eight categories of developmental behavior are surveyed: Ambulation, Manipulation, Rapport, Communication, Responsibility, Information, Ideation, and Creativity. For each category there is 1 item for each age period; these range by half-year intervals from birth to 84 months. Operational definitions are given in the manual for each item. For example, the definition for "Dresses Self" (placed under Responsibility) is: "unfastens and removes and/or replaces and fastens most of own garments without help or undue delay; washes and dries hands and face acceptably; need not tie laces, brush hair, or put on rubbers."
Scoring is in terms of Satisfactory, Intermittent or Marginal, and Unsatisfactory. The total score is expressed in months and

gives an Attainment Age that can be translated to an Attainment Quotient. A profile shows results for all items. A page is also included in the record booklet for environmental notes, family data, etc. The PAR is an extension of principles used in the Vineland Social Maturity Scale and is considered to have special usefulness for those individuals who are not accessible to direct examination because of various handicapping problems and to those who have cultural differences that reflect environmental stimulation deprivation or disadvantage. It permits comparisons of child with child or a given child with himself in successive measures; it may also be used for composing homogeneous groups or assessing their comparability.

NORMS, RELIABILITY, VALIDITY: None available

SOURCE: American Guidance Service, Inc., Publisher's Building, Circle Pines, Minnesota 55014

APPROXIMATE COST: $5 for Manual and 25 Record Blanks

Preschool and Kindergarten Performance Profile

AUTHORS: Alfred J. DiNola, Bernard P. Kaminsky, and Allen E. Sternfeld

DATE: 1970

PURPOSE: To identify pupils lacking in specific areas of development; to determine readiness of a pupil for new learning

AGE RANGE: Preschool and kindergarten

WHO CAN ADMINISTER: Teachers who have studied the manual

TIME TO ADMINISTER: Unspecified (rating scale)

DESCRIPTION: The Performance Profile consists of 50 items grouped under 3 major areas. A total of 10 topics are covered:

1. Social (Interpersonal Relations, Emotional Behavior, and Safety)
2. Intellectual (Communication, Basic Concepts, Perceptual Development, and Imagination and Creative Expression)
3. Physical (Self-Help, Gross Motor Skills, and Fine Visual Motor Skills)

The teacher rates each item according to a 7-point sequential scale. For example, descriptions for the question concerning

"Hazard Awareness" range from "Needs continuous cautioning" to "Is responsible for own safety and is concerned about others." Scores for the 10 topics may be shown on a profile sheet. A Progress Report Folder is provided to show individual development over several reporting periods.

NORMS, RELIABILITY, VALIDITY: None reported in manual

SOURCE: Educational Performance Associates, Inc., 463 Westview Avenue, Ridgefield, New Jersey 07657

APPROXIMATE COST: $6 for Manual, 1 Record Booklet, and 1 Progress Folder

Pre-School Screening Instrument (P.S.S.I.)

AUTHOR: Stephen P. Cohen

DATE: 1979

PURPOSE: To detect children with potential learning disabilities prior to comprehensive diagnostic testing

AGE RANGE: 4 to 5 years

WHO CAN ADMINISTER: Teachers, student teachers, teachers' aides, and others who have participated in a 3-hour workshop

TIME TO ADMINISTER: 5 to 8 minutes

DESCRIPTION: This instrument surveys the following areas:

1. Visual Motor Perception/Fine Motor (**Ex:** Child copies circle, cross, and square; reproduces block design and block tower)
2. Gross Motor (**Ex:** Child follows instructions to jump, hop, balance on one foot, throw and catch a ball)
3. Language Development (**Ex:** Child tells name, tells what he/she sees in a picture, and defines several verbs and nouns)
4. Drawing of a Person (supplementary subtest)

Instructions and illustrations are provided for scoring the subtests; raw scores can be converted to an "Estimated Range of Developmental Level." Clearness of speech is rated on a 3-point scale and behavior during testing is rated on a 5-point checklist (overactivity, etc.). The child is then placed in one of several categories, which indicates need for further evaluation or placement. A suggested letter to parents and a Parental Questionnaire containing 32 Yes-No items are included in the 36-

page manual. A sample parent-feedback letter is also provided.

NORMS, RELIABILITY, VALIDITY: Information available
SOURCE: Stoelting Company, 1350 South Kostner Avenue, Chicago, Illinois 60623
APPROXIMATE COST: $35 for Manual, 25 Student Record Books, 16 Wooden Blocks, Picture Story Card, Ball and 6 Kindergarten Size Pencils

Preschool Screening System: Start of a Longitudinal-Preventive Approach (Field Trial Edition)

AUTHORS: Peter K. Hainsworth and Marian L. Hainsworth
DATE: 1974
PURPOSE: To survey the learning skills of entering kindergarten or nursery school children so that curriculum may be better oriented toward their needs
AGE RANGE: 4-4 to 5-4 years
WHO CAN ADMINISTER: Teachers who have studied the manual (parent completes a questionnaire)
TIME TO ADMINISTER: 15 to 20 minutes
DESCRIPTION: The screening procedures consist of a test administered to the child and a Developmental Questionnaire completed by the parent. Part A of the child's test includes information processing skills that involve items grouped under the headings of movement patterns, clapping, following body directions, finger patterns, copying shapes, following spatial directions, quantity recognition, reading shapes, visual integration, serial counting, repeating phrases, and repeating sentences. Part B consists of drawing a person, and Part C has items pertaining to verbal reasoning (**Ex:** "Suzie is a girl. Bill is a . . ."). The examiner also completes a test observation section consisting of a 7-item checklist that covers such behaviors as speech, eye control, and hand use.

The Developmental Questionnaire for parents asks for data regarding school, family, medical, and developmental history. There are also 27 items grouped under the following headings: Play; How does your child dress self? Self-care at the table; When Talking; What TV does your child watch? Listening to stories being read; and Behavior. Each item is followed by a checklist with several choices.

Raw scores on both the child's test and the parent's questionnaire can be translated to percentiles for each of several areas. Results are to be transferred to a school list that shows each child's data summarized by use of these percentiles. The 81-page manual discusses follow-up of screening data and gives suggestions for translating data into initial program action. Additional material is available for program planning.

NORMS, RELIABILITY, VALIDITY: Manual provides information
SOURCE: Preschool Screening System, P. O. Box 1635, Pawtucket, Rhode Island 02862
APPROXIMATE COST: $16 for Manual, 50 Child's Record Forms, 50 Parent's Developmental Questionnaires

Preschool Screening Test

AUTHORS: Developed by Fort Worth Independent School District
DATE: 1974
PURPOSE: To identify children who may need special help in public school
AGE RANGE: Kindergarten to first grade
WHO CAN ADMINISTER: Professional school staff members who have studied the manual and volunteers who have attended a 2- to 3-hour workshop on administering the instrument
TIME TO ADMINISTER: 2 hours to screen 25 children (team administered)
DESCRIPTION: The Preschool Screening Test requires a team of 7 (1 professional and 6 volunteers) to screen 10 children at one time. The instrument uses a station approach; some items are administered individually and some are administered as a group. The test is divided into three sections:

Section I (20 minutes per child)
1. Memory (Auditory Long-Term, Auditory Immediate, Visual Long-Term, Visual Immediate)
2. Understanding Language (Auditory, Visual)
3. Closure (Auditory, Visual)
4. Communication (Manual, Verbal)

5. Relationships (Visual, Auditory)
Section II (10 minutes)
Motor (Fine-motor items are administered as a group)
Section III (3 minutes per child)
Motor (Fine and gross motor tasks are administered individually)

The 51-page manual provides instructions for administering, scoring, and interpreting test results.
NORMS, RELIABILITY, VALIDITY: Manual provides information
SOURCE: Fort Worth Independent School District, Department of Curriculum, Fort Worth, Texas
APPROXIMATE COST: Available from above source

Psycho-Educational Battery (PEB)

AUTHOR: Lillie Pope
DATE: 1977
PURPOSE: To help improve educational planning for individual learners by providing performance data that enables the teacher to pinpoint the needs of the individual
AGE RANGE: Level Y: Kindergarten to sixth grade
    Level O: Seventh grade to adult
WHO CAN ADMINISTER: Trained clinicians or specialists, teachers who have studied the test manual or who have attended a workshop on administration
TIME TO ADMINISTER: 2 hours
DESCRIPTION: The 20-page Evaluator's Recording Form for Level Y of the PEB contains 22 units, each of which includes several items. Whether all units are included depends on performance on other units. Some of the units usually used at the kindergarten level are: Gross Motor Performance, Fine Motor Coordination, Awareness of Place and Time, Knowledge of Left and Right, Tactile and Kinesthetic Perception, Knowledge of Reversible Words, and Tendency to Reverse.

The 60-page manual includes instruction for administration and scoring, but the author emphasizes that the quality of the evaluation depends on the skills of the observer. A final summary table of the units reflects the teacher's judgment on a 3-point scale ranging from "Student seems competent" to "Has yet to learn." There is space provided for comments on educational strategies and teaching techniques for each unit. An additional unit concerns behavior and learning style and consists of a checklist of "Handicapping Behaviors" and "Helpful Characteristics." These are rated on a 5-point scale ranging from Outstanding to Needs Further Investigation. There is also a 6-page parent interview form to be used to obtain information on family, social, and medical history.

The final outcome of the evaluator's report is to be an educational plan for the child, and the manual provides alternative forms for preparing this plan. A bibliography of books that contain remedial suggestions is included.

NORMS, RELIABILITY, VALIDITY: None reported in manual
SOURCE: Book-Lab, Inc., 1449 37th Street, Brooklyn, New York 11218
APPROXIMATE COST: $7 for Specimen Set

Psychoeducational Evaluation of the Preschool Child

AUTHORS: Eleonora Jedrysek, Zelda Klapper, Lillie Pope, and Joseph Wortis
DATE: 1972
PURPOSE: To evaluate the educational potential of preschool children in order that the teacher-evaluator can develop an appropriate curriculum for the individual child
AGE RANGE: 1 to 6 years
WHO CAN ADMINISTER: Child development workers, teachers, psychologists, nurses, and others who work with young children in or around the educational situation
TIME TO ADMINISTER: 2 hours (may be spread over several sessions)
DESCRIPTION: This educational evaluation instrument utilizes the Haeuessermann approach. There are 51 test items grouped under 5 areas of functioning:

1. Physical Function and Sensory Status (tasks that evaluate manual, visual, and auditory abilities)
2. Perceptual Functioning (such tasks as matching various types of material, copying designs with a pencil, fitting parts together)

3. Competence in Learning for Short-Term Retention (delayed recognition of forms, recall of a missing picture, repetition of digits and words, etc.)
4. Language Competence (such tasks as identification and recognition of objects, obeying commands, and giving verbal responses to questions)
5. Cognitive Functioning (items concerning concepts of number, amount, space, and size; memory for numbers and words, etc.)

Procedures for administering and scoring are in the 91-page manual. Most of the information on test items may be observed from activities in the classroom, but individual probing may be necessary for puzzling aspects of a child's performance. Probing procedures are included with test items.

The manual provides several examples of test records with school reports. These include observational comments and suggestions by teachers, recommendations for follow-up, and educational planning.

Norms, Reliability, Validity: None reported in manual
Source: Grune & Stratton, 111 Fifth Avenue, New York, New York 10003
Approximate Cost: $25 for Manual and 50 Test Forms

Pupil Record of Educational Behavior (PREB)

Author: Ruth Cheves
Date: 1975
Purpose: To evaluate a student's level and pattern of functioning in order to develop educational programs appropriate to individual needs
Age Range: Preschool to upper primary levels
Who can Administer: Teachers, clinicians, psychologists, diagnosticians, and other specialists who have studied the manual
Time to Administer: 30 minutes to 2 hours, depending on the number of tasks presented
Description: The PREB consists of 58 basic tasks in 4 general areas of performance:

1. Visual-Motor Perception (copying geometric forms, coloring

and cutting, reproducing pegboard designs, writing, following directions, etc.)

2. Auditory Perception (identifying letters, recognizing beginning consonant sounds, rhyming, etc.)

3. Language Development (matching letters, sequencing, defining words, etc.)

4. Mathematical Concepts (matching numbers, counting, problem solving, etc.)

Also included are 172 optional tasks for further evaluation. The teacher's guide gives instructions for recording observations in a 24-page pupil record booklet. Numerical scores are not given because emphasis is on exploring how each task is approached and recording qualitative, descriptive information about the child's level and pattern of functioning. The teacher's guide also includes discussion of use of the observations for educational programming or remedial teaching.

NORMS, RELIABILITY, VALIDITY: None reported in the manual
SOURCE: Teaching Resources Corporation, 100 Boylston Street, Boston, Massachusetts 02116
APPROXIMATE COST: $65 for Teacher's Guide, 15 Pupil Record Booklets, and Manipulative Materials; a Spanish Edition is available

Quick Neurological Screening Test (QNST)

AUTHORS: Margret Mutti, Harold M. Sterling, Norma V. Spalding
DATE: 1974
PURPOSE: To screen for possible developmental or neurological interferences that could affect learning
AGE RANGE: Kindergarten through twelfth grade
WHO CAN ADMINISTER: Psychologists, other specialists, and school personnel who have studied the manual; authors suggest a minumum of 25 practice tests for competence
TIME TO ADMINISTER: 20 minutes
DESCRIPTION: The QNST consists of 14 subtests. These are named below, with a brief description of the tasks involved in each.

1. Hand Skill (**Ex:** Child writes name)

2. Figure Recognition and Production (**Ex:** Child names and copies 6 geometric forms)
3. Rapid Hand Movements (**Ex:** Child repeats simple hand movements of examiner)
4. Palm Form Recognition (**Ex:** With eyes closed, child identifies number written on palm)
5. Finger to Nose (**Ex:** Child follows several instructions by examiner, which include touching nose with eyes closed)
6. Thumb and Finger Circle (**Ex:** Child repeats examiner's demonstration)
7. Double-Simultaneous Stimulation of Hand and Cheek (**Ex:** With eyes closed, child reports location of series of light touches)
8. Eye Tracking (**Ex:** Child follows an object with the eyes)
9. Sound Patterns (**Ex:** With eyes closed, child repeats examiner's patterns of clapping)
10. Arm and Leg Extension (**Ex:** Child follows instructions of examiner who observes for tremor and other abnormalities)
11. Tandem Walk (**Ex:** Child walks an imaginary straight line)
12. Stand and Skip (**Ex:** Child follows instructions with eyes open and eyes closed)
13. Left-Right Discrimination (**Ex:** Performance on subtests 5, 6, and 12 are scored for mirroring)
14. Behavioral Irregularities (**Ex:** Examiner scores for 6 types of behavior such as "excessive talking")

Each subtest is scored according to several specific criteria that are described on the scoring form. The total score indicates whether the child may be considered neurologically normal. The manual includes a discussion of the rationale and importance of each of the 14 tasks, educational implications, medical aspects, and an extensive bibliography.

NORMS, RELIABILITY, VALIDITY: Manual provides information
SOURCE: Academic Therapy Publications, 20 Commercial Boulevard, Novato, California 94947
APPROXIMATE COST: $14 for Manual and 25 Recording Forms

Rhode Island Pupil Identification Scale (RIPIS)

AUTHORS: Harry S. Novack, Elisa Bonaventura, Peter Merenda

Date: 1973
Purpose: To identify children with learning problems
Age Range: 4 through 7 years
Who can Administer: Teachers who have studied the manual and who have observed the child in the classroom for a month or more
Time to Administer: Unspecified (checklist)
Description: This scale consists of a 5-page test form that contains 40 items divided into 2 parts:

1. Part 1 consists of 21 items regarding child behaviors that can normally be observed in the classroom (**Ex:** "Fails to take reprimands well")
2. Part 2 deals with behavior that is most readily observable through written work (**Ex:** "Has difficulty staying within lines when coloring")

The teacher rates the child's behavior on each item on a scale ranging from 1 (Never) to 5 (Always). The higher the scores the more learning difficulties a child is expected to experience.
Norms, Reliability, Validity: Manual provides information
Source: R.I.P.I.S., P. O. Box 9311, Providence, Rhode Island 02940
Approximate Cost: $13 for Manual and 35 Test Forms

School/Home Observation & Referral System (SHORS)

Author: Joyce Evans
Date: 1978
Purpose: To identify children with problems that may interfere with learning
Age Range: Preschool age through third grade
Who can Administer: Parents, teachers, assistant teachers, and other professionals who work with young children and who have studied the manual
Time to Administer: Unspecified (checklist)
Description: The SHORS consists of a parent's guide and a teacher's Observation & Referral Record, which contain somewhat similar checklists that are grouped according to 7 areas of functioning:

1. Health (**Ex:** "Is frequently sick or seems to be in poor health")
2. Motor (**Ex:** "Does not use toys or other objects as easily as others")
3. Vision (**Ex:** "Rubs eyes frequently")
4. Hearing (**Ex:** "Does not react to sudden or loud noises")
5. Speech & Language (**Ex:** "Does not talk")
6. Learning (**Ex:** "Is unusually slow or has difficulty in learning")
7. Behavior (**Ex:** "Clings to adults")

The teacher's record contains a brief 18-item checklist that indicates which of the 7 areas should be evaluated in more detail. For this purpose, there are 7 additional checklists that require more detailed evaluation of the area in question. Each of these checklists contains 20 to 30 items grouped under headings of Appearance, Behavior, and Related Problems, with space provided for other observation or information.

The 13-page parent's guide provides a general discussion of each area of functioning and a 4-page checklist that is to be filled in by the parents, torn out, and returned to the teacher. The guide encourages the parent to talk to the teacher about problems in order to find out whether the child seems to have the same problems at school.

A 56-page teacher's guide gives detailed information, interpretive comments, and suggestions for follow-up for each area of functioning. The teacher uses this information and results of the teacher's and parent's checklists to determine need for conferring with parents and other staff members. The combined information helps the teacher make effective referrals so that recommendations for teatment and remediation may be instituted. Additional orientation materials for teachers and parents are available.

NORMS, RELIABILITY, VALIDITY: Information available
SOURCE: CTB/McGraw-Hill, Del Monte Research Park, Monterey, California 93940
APPROXIMATE COST: $55 for Teacher's Guide, 30 Observation & Referral Records, Parent's Guides, 4 each of 7 Specific Checklists

Southeastern Day Care Project Rating Scales

AUTHORS: Staff of the Southeastern Day Care Project, Nancy E. Travis, Director

DATE: 1973

PURPOSE: To help day care staff assess children in order to individualize programs for each child

AGE RANGE: Birth to 6 years

WHO CAN ADMINISTER: Day care staff who have studied the manual and have been trained by program directors

TIME TO ADMINISTER: Unspecified (rating scale)

DESCRIPTION: The Rating Scales consist of a total of 60 items divided according to 4 age groups (birth to 30 months, age 2, age 3, and age 4 to 6). Items in each age scale are grouped according to 4 areas shown below; examples are for the 3 to 4 year level:

1. Cognitive (**Ex:** "Uses plurals")
2. Social and Emotional (**Ex:** "Knows and relates to own sex")
3. Motor Skills (**Ex:** "Walks down stairs")
4. Hygiene and Self-Help (**Ex:** "Washes hands")

Each item includes a brief explanation to help the rater mark Yes or No; the manual provides additional interpretations and examples. The first rating should be carried out shortly after a child enters the day care center and additional ratings can be done frequently. For example, for 2-year-olds the rating form should be repeated at 4-month intervals. The authors urge that ratings be carried out in a flexible manner as the behavior occurs spontaneously or in the context of a game or planned activity. Rating may be done by one teacher or by several staff members. Results are not to be used as test scores but should be used to help the staff understand some of the objectives of the day care center and to plan individual and group programs with these objectives in mind.

NORMS, RELIABILITY, VALIDITY: None reported in manual

SOURCE: Day Care and Child Development Council of America, Inc., 1012 - 14th street NW, Washington, D. C. 20005

APPROXIMATE COST: $5 for the Manual. Test forms in the manual may be copied.

Valett Developmental Survey of Basic Learning Abilities

AUTHOR: Robert E. Valett
DATE: 1966
PURPOSE: To evaluate various developmental abilities of children in order to help plan individualized learning programs
AGE RANGE: 2 to 7 years
WHO CAN ADMINISTER Teachers who have studied the manual
TIME TO ADMINISTER: Unspecified
DESCRIPTION: The Survey consists of 233 items listed by age level. These items were compiled from various developmental sources. They are listed in sequential order with sources indicated, under 7 areas of development. Examples below are at the 4-year level:

1. Motor Integration and Physical Development (**Ex:** "Throw me the ball.")
2. Tactile Discrimination (**Ex:** "Put your hand in the bag and find me the spoon.")
3. Auditory Discrimination (**Ex:** "Say, 'We are going to buy some candy for mother.' ")
4. Visual-Motor Coordination (**Ex:** "Draw me a picture like this.")
5. Visual Discrimination (**Ex:** "Show me one like this.")
6. Language Development and Verbal Fluency (**Ex:** "What burns?")
7. Conceptual Development (**Ex:** "Give me two pennies.")

Most of the testing materials are described in the manual as easily available to teachers. Scoring is according to Correct, Incorrect, or Partial accomplishment. Range of developmental level is estimated for each area; strengths and weaknesses are noted for the purpose of helping plan an educational program. Additional materials are available for diagnosing and remediation of learning disabilities.

NORMS, RELIABILITY, VALIDITY: None reported in manual
SOURCE: Consulting Psychologists Press, Inc., 577 College Avenue, Palo Alto, California 94306
APPROXIMATE COST: $19 for Manual, Card Set, and 25 Workbooks and Scoring Booklets

Vineland Social Maturity Scale

AUTHOR: Edgar A. Doll
DATE: 1965, Fourth Edition
PURPOSE: To measure successive stages of social competence
AGE RANGE: Infancy to 25 years or older
WHO CAN ADMINISTER: Teachers, clinicians, specialists, and trained paraprofessionals who have studied the manual and the book, *Measurement of Social Competence* (interpretation should be done by clinicians, school psychologists, and other testing specialists)
TIME TO ADMINISTER: 30 minutes
DESCRIPTION: This scale is completed by an interviewer who obtains the required information from someone intimately familiar with the person scored. The subject need not be present or observed but under certain conditions the subject may be used as his/her own informant. The 117 items on the scale are arranged in order of increasing difficulty and are divided into groups according to age periods. The items are also designated as representing 1 of 6 maturational areas: Self-Help, Self-Direction, Occupation, Communication, Locomotion, and Socialization. The interviewer begins with items below the child's anticipated age level score and stops when it is clear that items are beyond the subject's competence. Interviewing and scoring must be carried out according to specific instructions in the manual. The final score is in terms of Social Age; this Social Age may be divided by the chronological age to obtain a Social Quotient. According to the publishers, a revised edition will be published in late 1981.
NORMS, RELIABILITY, VALIDITY: Information available
SOURCE: American Guidance Service, Inc., Publishers' Building, Circle Pines, Minnesota 35014
APPROXIMATE COST: $4 for Manual and 25 Record Blanks; $8 for *Measurement of Social Competence*

Visco Child Development Screening Test (ChilDSTest)

AUTHORS: Susan J. Visco and Carmela R. Visco
DATE: 1978
PURPOSE: To identify children who might be at risk for special

learning needs

Age Range: 3 to 7 years

Who can Administer: Teachers who have studied the instruction manual and have had in-service training

Time to Aminister: 25 to 30 minutes

Description: This screening device consists of 115 items grouped under 12 subtests. Tasks for each subtest become increasingly difficult. The subtests are listed below:

1. Fine Motor Skills (**Ex:** Child is directed to perform tasks involving use of fingers and/or hand, such as buttoning four buttons)
2. Gross Motor Skills (**Ex:** Child is asked to hop, jump, walk a line, etc.)
3. Visual Sequencing: Body Direction (**Ex:** Examiner demonstrates finger, hand, and foot patterns which the child then imitates)
4. Auditory Sequencing: Body Direction (**Ex:** Child is requested to touch specified body parts, etc.)
5. Copy Figures (**Ex:** Child copies nine geometric figures)
6. Perceptuomotor: Spatial Directions (**Ex:** Examiner requests child to make drawings such as "a circle *above* the box.")
7. Auditory Sequencing (**Ex:** Child repeats phrases and sentences after the examiner)
8. Numerical Counting (**Ex:** Examiner asks child to count to 10 forward and backward and by 2s)
9. Numerical Gestalt (**Ex:** Examiner exposes for 1 to 5 seconds cards that contain varying numbers of dots; child indicates number of dots)
10. Draw-a-Picture (**Ex:** Child makes a drawing and then is asked to name the drawing)
11. Language (**Ex:** Examiner uses 25 picture cards and asks for name of each object and its function)
12. Articulation (**Ex:** Child repeats 54 words after examiner; substitutions, omissions, etc., are noted but not scored)

Scores for each subtest except Articulation are shown on a summary sheet. Scores can be translated to Possible, Low, Moderate, or High Risk for special needs, and the manual provides suggestions for further interpretation of the subtests.

Additional forms at the end of the Record Booklet include a Teacher Observation Report (a checklist of general classroom behavior), an Examiner Observation Form, and a Parent Report of family and infant history and of developmental milestones.

NORMS, RELIABILITY, VALIDITY: Information provided in the Overview Manual

SOURCE: Educational Activities, Inc., Freeport, New York 11520

APPROXIMATE COST: $39 for Manuals, 20 Record Booklets, and test materials

Windsor Early Identification Project

AUTHOR: K. G. O'Bryan

DATE: 1976

PURPOSE: To identify children unlikely to cope with the beginning school experience, as well as extremely capable children who might need programs especially adapted to their exceptional abilities

AGE RANGE: Several months before entrance to kindergarten and immediately before entrance (2 stages)

WHO CAN ADMINISTER: Teachers who have studied the manual (parent involvement is required)

TIME TO ADMINISTER: 45 minutes

DESCRIPTION: The first stage of administration occurs in the spring prior to the child's entrance to kindergarten. The parent visits the school with the child and provides basic social history to help the school secretary complete the first half of the social history form. In September the parent and child return to school and meet the kindergarten teacher; the teacher and parent together complete the social and health history form. This section deals with personal data concerning the child. When the interview is completed, the teacher begins the assessment procedure, using materials that are inexpensive and easily available. At this time the child is tested for Color Recognition, Receptive Language, Expressive Language, Auditory Association, and Mathematics Skills. Then during the first weeks of school, the teacher completes a behavioral assessment and compiles anecdotal records. Speech, hearing, and vision are tested early in the year; if any problems are identified, the information is relayed to parents and teacher. Children who are identified by the procedures as "at-risk" are referred to an appropriate consultant.

NORMS, RELIABILITY, VALIDITY: Manual provides information
SOURCE: The Ontario Institute for Studies in Education, Publication Sales, 252 Bloor Street West, Toronto, Ontario
APPROXIMATE COST: $3 for the Manual

Yellow Brick Road

AUTHOR: Christine Kallstrom
DATE: 1975
PURPOSE: To identify preschool children's strengths and weaknesses in basic functioning
AGE RANGE: 3 to 6 years
WHO CAN ADMINISTER: Teachers who have studied the manual or attended a workshop; clinicians or specialists; trained volunteers, aides, and parents who may assist (examiners should have at least one practice session)
TIME TO ADMINISTER: 45 minutes
DESCRIPTION: This screening instrument consists of game-like tasks that follow the *Wizard of Oz* theme. A separate station for each of 4 test batteries is set up. Stations are given the labels of Scarecrow, Lion, Tin Man, and Munchkins, and the child is issued "Admission Tickets." There are 6 subtests for each of the 4 stations:

1. Motor (imitation, movement, body parts, spatial relationships, right-left, draw-a-person)
2. Visual (tracking, fusion, visual discrimination, visual memory, visual motor, figure-ground)
3. Auditory (auditory discrimination, sequencing, automatic associations, etc.)
4. Language (motor encoding, vocal encoding, categories, articulation, conversation, etc.)

Scoring is based on pass-fail on each item and suggestions are given as to whether total scores indicate adequate functioning according to age level. The author encourages caution in making interpretations, but says the possibility of referral should be considered for children with inadequate functioning. The manual contains developmental activities that can be used to train children to develop skills in each area.

NORMS, RELIABILITY, VALIDIY: Manual provides information
SOURCE: Teaching Resources Corporation, 50 Pond Park Road, Hingham, Massachusetts 02043
APPROXIMATE COST: $40 for Manual, 4 Battery Booklets, Testing Materials, and 25 Admission Tickets

Zeitlin Early Identification Screening (ZEIS)

AUTHOR: Shirley Zeitlin
DATE: 1975
PURPOSE: To identify early kindergarten and prekindergarten children who may have special learning needs
AGE RANGE: 3 to 7 years
WHO CAN ADMINISTER: Teachers, paraprofessionals, and other educational personnel after one training session
TIME TO ADMINISTER: 15 to 20 minutes
DESCRIPTION: The ZEIS may be given entirely by 1 examiner or by the use of 3 separate stations in a room. There are 3 to 5 items (**Ex:** "Show me the cat in this picture") in each of 12 sections: Information, Vocabulary, Language, Auditory Memory, Concepts, Draw a Person, Copy Forms, Recall, Directions, Gross Motor, Body Image, Directions - Imitation, and Directions - Verbal. Specific instructions and illustrations for scoring are given. Summarized results are to be shown on the first page of the test form under headings of Verbal, Pencil and Paper, and Performance. There is also a checklist on this page for the examiner to indicate 8 types of characteristics shown during testing (agile-clumsy, attentive-inattentive, etc.). Guidelines are given for interpretation of results; for example, children whose scores place them in the lower 10 percent of the group tested may need diagnostic follow-through. Since the ZEIS is a research edition and may be duplicated, the author requests that users share results with her.

NORMS, RELIABILITY, VALIDITY: Information available

SOURCE: Shirley Zeitlin, van den Berg Center, State University College, New Paltz, New York 12561

APPROXIMATE COST: Available from above source

Category 3

LANGUAGE/BILINGUAL

Assessment of Children's Language Comprehension (ACLC)

AUTHORS: Rochana Foster, Jane J. Giddan, and Joel Stark
DATE: 1972
PURPOSE: To assess receptive language difficulties in young children and to indicate guidelines for correction of language disorders (a group form is for screening only)
AGE RANGE: 3 to 6-6 years
WHO CAN ADMINISTER: Teachers and paraprofessionals who have attended a workshop on administration (interpretation should be by a clinician, school psychologist, or other testing specialist)
TIME TO ADMINISTER: 10 to 20 minutes
DESCRIPTION: The ACLC was designed to determine how many word classes, in different combinations of length and complexity, a child can comprehend. The examiner states the word or phrase and the child points to the appropriate picture. Part A consists of testing for a core vocabulary of 50 words. If the child fails this part, the other parts are not administered until the child has had the chance to increase his/her vocabulary. Part B consists of phrases with two critical elements, such as "big shoe." Part C consists of phrases with three critical elements, such as "girl blowing the horn." Part D involves four critical elements, such as "boy standing in the house." The ACLC is essentially an achievement or criterion-referenced test but mean scores are given by age and sex in the 32-page manual. The manual also includes discussion of language impairment and gives guidelines for language training and clinical applications of the ACLC.

A shorter group form has been developed for screening small groups of children such as those in kindergarten programs. This form, containing 12 items, can be administered by teachers and teacher aides who have studied the manual. It

79

consists of 17 plates in an individual 32-page booklet. The child marks the correct picture of the phrase stated by the examiner. If fewer than 9 items are correctly marked, the child should be tested individually on the full ACLC or other diagnostic instruments.

NORMS, RELIABILITY, VALIDITY: Manual provides information

SOURCE: Consulting Psychologists Press, Inc., 577 College Avenue, Palo Alto, California 94306

APPROXIMATE COST: $14 for the 40-card booklet and pad of 50 Recording Sheets

Basic Inventory of Natural Language (BINL)

AUTHOR: Charles H. Herbert

DATE: 1977

PURPOSE: To determine language dominance, proficiency, and reading placement and to help individualize language reading instruction in Spanish and English

AGE RANGE: Kindergarten through grade 12

WHO CAN ADMINISTER: Teachers or teacher aides who have received the 1-day training workshop developed by the publisher

TIME TO ADMINISTER: Unspecified (administration should be preceded by one to five 20-minute group-practice sessions with a tape recorder)

DESCRIPTION: This is a criterion-referenced test, with scores derived from tape recorded samples taken during a structured, small-group language activity. Elementary and secondary level kits contain 3 types of stimulus materials for individual stories. The materials include 40 full-color Story Starter posters, 60 Talk Tiles (small drawings mounted on cardboard), and Story Sequence Pictures (a ditto master book of sequence picture stories to be mounted on cardboard). During practice sessions and actual testing sessions, the students choose several pictures each and take turns describing or telling stories about the pictures they have selected. After students have become familiar with the activities, a sample of each student's oral language, consisting of at least 10 partial and/or complete sentences, is taken as part of the classroom activities. The tape-recorded sample is then transcribed onto the score sheet and scored either by hand or by machine. Based on an analysis of the samples, language development activities may be prescribed by the teacher. Prescription activities, some of which employ the materials provided for practice and testing, are described in the manual.

NORMS, RELIABILITY, VALIDITY: Information available

SOURCE: CHECpoint Systems, Inc., 1520 North Waterman Avenue, San Bernardino, California 92404

APPROXIMATE COST: $75 for testing materials, Manual, 400 Score Sheets, and 200 Profile Sheets

Bilingual Syntax Measure

AUTHORS: Marina Burt, Heidi C. Dulay, and Eduardo Hernandez Ch.

DATE: 1975

PURPOSE: To measure oral proficiency in English and/or Spanish grammatical structures

AGE RANGE: 4 to 9 years

WHO CAN ADMINISTER: Teachers, school evaluators, and other qualified personnel who have studied the manual and are fluent in the language used (Spanish or English)

TIME TO ADMINISTER: 10 to 16 minutes

DESCRIPTION: The Bilingual Syntax Measure does not assess pronunciation, vocabulary range, or scope of information, but measures the child's control of the basic English or Spanish grammatical structures used to express ideas and opinions in ordinary communication. The test consists of 23 items, each involving a picture stimulus. For example, the administrator points to a picture of baby birds and asks, "What are these?" The grammatical response might be "ducks" and the ungrammatical response might be "duck." Instructions are given in the manual for evaluating and scoring responses. The total score is transformed to 1 of 5 proficiency levels. For English these are No English, Receptive English only, Survival English, Intermediate English, and Proficient English. Students who take both the English and the Spanish versions can be classified according to their degree of structural bilingualism or language dominance. The manual includes instructional suggestions for working with children at each of the proficiency levels.

NORMS, RELIABILITY, VALIDITY: Manual and Technical Report provide detailed information

SOURCE: The Psychological Corporation, 757 Third Avenue, New York, New York 10017

APPROXIMATE COST: $55 for the Picture Booklet, Child Response Booklets (35 in English and 35 in Spanish), English Manual, Spanish Manual, Class Records, Technical Handbook, and Storage Box

The Bzoch-League Receptive Expressive-Emergent Language Scale (REEL)

AUTHORS: Kenneth R. Bzoch and Richard League

DATE: 1970-71

PURPOSE: To measure receptive and expressive language skills in very young children and to detect handicaps in language acquisition

AGE RANGE: Birth to 3 years

WHO CAN ADMINISTER: Teachers and teacher aides who have studied the manual

TIME TO ADMINISTER: 10 to 15 minutes

DESCRIPTION: The REEL Scale consists of 132 items requiring a Yes-No response and can usually be completed through an interview with the mother or principal caretaker. There are 6 items for each month for the first year, 6 items for each 2-month interval for the second year, and 6 items for each 4-month period for the third year. Half the items deal with receptive language and half deal with expressive language. A receptive item is "Appears to understand some new words each week." An expressive item at the same (12 to 14 month) level is "Uses 5 or more true words with some consistency." Three language quotients (expressive, receptive, and combined) are derived. The manual includes a discussion of language acquisition.

NORMS, RELIABILITY, VALIDITY: Information available

SOURCE: University Park Press, 233 East Redwood Street, Baltimore, Maryland 21202

Approximate Cost: $10 for Manual and $7 for 25 forms

Child Language Ability Measures (CLAM)

Author: Albert Mehrabian
Date: 1970
Purpose: To measure child's language comprehension and production
Age Range: 2 through 6 years
Who can Administer: Teachers who have studied the manual and paraprofessionals who have been trained to administer the instrument
Time to Administer: 20 to 35 minutes depending on number of subtests administered
Description: The CLAM consists of six subtests:

1. Vocabulary Comprehension (45 items). (**Ex:** Examiner names an object and child responds by pointing to one of four pictures.)
2. Grammar Comprehension (50 items). (**Ex:** Examiner shows several pictures and asks the child to point to a particular one, such as the one in which "The girl is the biggest.")
3. Inflection Production (40 items). (**Ex:** Examiner asks the child to supply the key missing word at the end of a description of one or more pictures, such as "Here are some children who like to dance. Everyday he dances. Everyday she dances. Everyday they both ———.")
4. Grammar Formedness Judgment (50 items). (**Ex:** Examiner says two phrases, such as "He fall down/He falls down," and the child repeats the phrase that "sounds better.")
5. Grammar Imitation (50 items). (**Ex:** Child repeats a sentence, such as "The boy's car is on the table." Scoring is based on whether a key portion is repeated in correct order.)
6. Grammar Equivalence Judgment (40 items). (**Ex:** Examiner says two short sentences such as "Pick the toy up/Pick up the toy" and the child says whether the meaning is the same or different.)

There are two administration booklets, one for the vocabulary and grammar comprehension subtests and one for the remaining 4 subtests. Scores on each subtest may be compared to tables showing median scores. The manual shows appropriate age range for each of the subtests, which may be used singly or in combination.

NORMS, RELIABILITY, VALIDITY: Manual provides information
SOURCE: Albert Mehrabian, 9305 Beverlycrest Drive, Beverly Hills, California 90210
APPROXIMATE COST: $52 for Manual and two Administration Booklets (Answer Sheets in Booklets may be copied for use by the test administrator)

Communicative Evaluation Chart From Infancy to Five Years

AUTHORS: Ruth M. Anderson, Madeline Niles, and Patricia A. Matheny
DATE: 1963
PURPOSE: To discover children with communicative disabilities who need to be referred to clinical services and early therapy
AGE RANGE: 3 months to 5 years
WHO CAN ADMINISTER: Teachers or parents who have read the instructions
TIME TO ADMINISTER: Unspecified (checklist)
DESCRIPTION: From 12 to 25 items are given for each of the following ages: 3 months, 6 months, 9 months, 1 year, 1 1/2 years, 2 years, 3 years, 4 years and 5 years. Half the items deal with the development and comprehension of language as a communicative tool (**Ex:** 3 months — "meaningful smile"; 2 years — "has discarded jargon"; 5 years — "speech is fully intelligible"); the other half deals with physical growth and development, motor coordination, and visual/motor responses (**Ex:** 3 months — "good digestion"; 2 years — "spontaneous scribble with a pencil"; 5 years — "hops on one foot for 10 to 12 feet"). Items on the checklist, which is in the form of a single-fold chart, have been taken from Gesell, Binet, Cattell, and others. Items are rated "present," "not present," or "fluctuating." Instructions for administration are printed on the chart.
NORMS, RELIABILITY, VALIDITY: None available
SOURCE: Educators Publishing Service, 75 Moulton Street, Cambridge, Massachusetts 02138

APPROXIMATE COST: $.30 for each Chart

Del Rio Language Screening Test (English/Spanish)

AUTHORS: Allen S. Toronto, D. Leverneau, Cornelia Hanna, Peggy Rosenweig, and Antoneta Maldonada
DATE: 1975
PURPOSE: To identify both English-dominant and Spanish-dominant young children who are in need of speech and language therapy
AGE RANGE: 3 to 6-11 years
WHO CAN ADMINISTER: Teachers who have studied the manual and paraprofessionals who have been trained to administer the instrument
TIME TO ADMINISTER: Unspecified
DESCRIPTION: This test is appropriate for 3 groups of children: English-speaking Anglo-Americans, predominantly English-speaking Mexican-Americans, and predominantly Spanish-speaking Mexican-Americans. There are 5 subtests: Receptive Vocabulary (flip cards are used with this subtest); Sentence Repetition—Length; Sentence Repetition—Complexity; Oral Commands; and Story Comprehension. Each may be used separately or in combination with other subtests and may be administered in English or in Spanish. If the child is bilingual, both the English and Spanish versions may be administered. Norms are provided for 4 age levels. The test may also be used to determine the bilingual child's proficiency in each language in order to ascertain proper placement in bilingual programs.
NORMS, RELIABILITY, VALIDITY: Manual provides detailed information
SOURCE: National Educational Laboratory Publishers, Inc., P. O. Box 1003 (813 Airport Boulevard), Austin, Texas 78702
APPROXIMATE COST: $15 for DRLST Kit which includes Manual, 30 English Scoring Forms, and 30 Spanish Scoring Forms

Dos Amigos Verbal Language Scales

AUTHOR: Donald E. Critchlow
DATE: 1974

PURPOSE: To assist in determining the comparative language development of the Mexican-American child and to screen for problems requiring further evaluation

AGE RANGE: 5-0 to 13-6 years

WHO CAN ADMINISTER: Any person who is able to speak and read both Spanish and English and who has a complete knowledge of the instructions for administering the scales (interpretation should be by a professional with a thorough knowledge of the entire manual)

TIME TO ADMINISTER: 20 minutes (10 minutes for each scale)

DESCRIPTION: The test includes two scales consisting of a list of 85 English words and a similar list of 85 Spanish words. These are arranged in order of difficulty. The examiner first determines that the child understands what an opposite is and then reads each word; the child is asked to respond with an opposite. Testing is stopped after 5 consecutive failures. Total correct scores are translated to percentiles for each language based on age. Suggestions are given for interpreting results. For example, children below the 50th percentile in both English and Spanish should be evaluated further. The author also discusses diagnostic applications and instructional planning.

NORMS, RELIABILITY, VALIDITY: Manual provides information

SOURCE: Academic Therapy Publications, 20 Commercial Boulevard, Novato, California 94947

APPROXIMATE COST: $8 for Manual and 25 Test Sheets

Hannah-Gardner Test of Verbal and Nonverbal Language Functioning

AUTHORS: Elaine P. Hannah and Julie C. Gardner

DATE: 1978

PURPOSE: To identify children with a language deficit to which some attention should be given

AGE RANGE: 3-6 to 5-6 years

WHO CAN ADMINISTER: Teachers and other professionals who have studied the manual

TIME TO ADMINISTER: 25 to 35 minutes

DESCRIPTION: This test consists of 42 items divided into 5 sections. The sections with brief descriptions are:

1. Visual Perception (**Ex:** Eight tasks that require the child to find pairs, fold a triangle, tell what is funny about a picture, etc.)
2. Conceptual Development (**Ex:** Twenty tasks such as counting blocks, identifying such concepts as "longer," finishing sentences, etc.)
3. Auditory Perception (**Ex:** Tasks such as following commands, answering questions, and placing cards according to the examiner's story.)
4. Linguistic Development, Reception (**Ex:** Five items that test knowledge of plural nouns and pronouns by requiring the child to point to pictures.)
5. Linguistic Development, Expression (**Ex:** Eight picture items that require the child to use words to indicate plurals, past tense, negation, etc.)

Raw scores and percentile ranks are recorded for each of the 5 categories on the score sheets. A total verbal and a total nonverbal score are computed separately. The examiner also indicates intelligibility of the child's speech on a 4-point scale ranging from "speech easily understood," to "completely unintelligible." A Spanish version of the testing material is available.

NORMS, RELIABILITY, VALIDITY: Manual provides information
SOURCE: Lingua Press, P. O. Box 293, Northridge, California 91324
APPROXIMATE COST: $50 for portfolio containing Manual, 25 Score Sheets, and test materials

Inventory of Language Abilities (ILA)

AUTHORS: Esther H. Minskoff, Douglas E. Wideman, and J. Gerald Minskoff
DATE: 1972
PURPOSE: To identify children with possible language learning disabilities
AGE RANGE: 4 to 7 years
WHO CAN ADMINISTER: Teachers who have studied the manual and have had at least six weeks to observe their students
TIME TO ADMINISTER: Unspecified (checklist)

DESCRIPTION: The ILA is based on the Illinois Test of Psycholinguistic Abilities and is a component of the MWM Program for Developing Language Abilities. The Record Book for each child includes directions for administering and scoring, a profile sheet, and a summary page. There are 12 items to be checked for each of 11 areas of functioning as indicated below:

1. Auditory Reception
2. Visual Reception
3. Auditory Association
4. Visual Association
5. Verbal Expression
6. Manual Expression
7. Auditory Memory
8. Visual Memory
9. Grammatic Closure
10. Visual Closure
11. Auditory Closure

If more than 50 percent of the twelve items in any subtest are checked, there is a possible learning disability in that area, and the authors recommend that the child should be referred for an individual diagnostic evaluation with the Illinois Test of Psycholinguistic Abilities and other tests to be administered by a qualified examiner. If this is not possible, the teacher should provide remediation using the MWM Program for Developing Language Abilities. Detailed instructions for remedial use of this program are given in a Teacher's Guide.

NORMS, RELIABILITY, VALIDITY: Information available
SOURCE: Educational Performance Associates, Ridgefield, New Jersey 07657
APPROXIMATE COST: $15 for 25 Record Booklets

James Language Dominance Test

AUTHOR: Peter James
DATE: 1974
PURPOSE: To assess the language dominance of Mexican-American children
AGE RANGE: Kindergarten and first grade
WHO CAN ADMINISTER: Professional or paraprofessional persons who have studied the manual and who are fluent in English and Spanish
TIME TO ADMINISTER: 10 minutes

DESCRIPTION: This test utilizes 40 pictures to assess the child's language comprehension and production in Spanish and in English. The test is first administered in Spanish and then in English. Twenty items are used in each of 2 parts, as indicated below for the Spanish version:

1. *Spanish Comprehension.* The examiner names a word in Spanish and the child points to the appropriate picture.
2. *Spanish Production.* As the examiner shows the child a pictorial illustration, he/she asks in Spanish, "What is this?" and the child responds in Spanish if possible.

The above procedure is then repeated with the examiner and the child speaking English. Alternate responses are acceptable on certain words as indicated in the instructions. Also, comprehension items that are missed by more than half the subjects tested may be excluded in the final tabulations. The manual includes instructions for classifying the child into 1 of 5 categories: Spanish dominant, bilingual with Spanish as a home language, bilingual with English as a home language, English dominant but bilingual in comprehension, English dominant.

NORMS, RELIABILITY, VALIDITY: Manual provides information
SOURCE: Teaching Resources Corporation, 50 Pond Park Road, Hingham, Massachusetts 02043
APPROXIMATE COST: $20 for Manual, 25 Scoring Booklets, and 1 Test Booklet containing the pictorial stimuli

Kindergarten Language Screening Test (KLST)

AUTHORS: Sharon V. Gauthier and Charles L. Madison
DATE: 1975
PURPOSE: To screen for language deficits
AGE RANGE: 4 through 6 years
WHO CAN ADMINISTER: Teachers who have studied the manual
TIME TO ADMINISTER: 5 minutes
DESCRIPTION: This test includes both receptive and expressive language tasks. These involve such items as identification of colors and body parts, knowledge of number concepts, ability to follow commands, and sentence repetition. A spontaneous speech sample is also obtained. A cut-off point for the total

score is used to indicate likelihood of later school problems and need for further diagnostic testing.

NORMS, RELIABILITY, VALIDITY: Manual provides information
SOURCE: C. C. Publications, Inc., P. O. Box 23699, Tigard, Oregon 97223
APPROXIMATE COST: $25 for portfolio containing Manual and 40 Test Forms

Language Assessment Battery (LAB)

AUTHORS: Prepared by New York City Board of Education
DATE: 1976
PURPOSE: To measure a student's mastery of English and Spanish
AGE RANGE: Kindergarten to second grade (Level I)
WHO CAN ADMINISTER: Teachers and other qualified school personnel who have studied the manual
TIME TO ADMINISTER: 5 to 10 minutes
DESCRIPTION: The LAB consists of 40 items that assess reading, writing, listening comprehension, and speaking. There is an English version and a Spanish version. Each version assesses the child's effectiveness in the following areas:

1. Listening and Speaking (**Ex:** "These are things you find at home. Name the object in the drawings that I'm going to touch.")
2. Reading (**Ex:** "Here is a picture and three words. Which word says what the picture shows?")
3. Writing (**Ex:** "Here is a letter of the alphabet. Write the letter on the line.")

Total number of items answered correctly can be translated to percentile ranks and stanines. Suggested cut-off points are given to help identify children who may be unable to participate in an English learning situation and to determine which children are more effective in Spanish than in English.

NORMS, RELIABILITY, VALIDITY: Technical Manual gives detailed information
SOURCE: Riverside Publishing Company, 1919 South Highland Avenue, Lombard, Illinois 60148
APPROXIMATE COST: $7 for either English or Spanish version of

Examiner's Directions, Picture Stimulus Booklet, and 35 Test Booklets

Language Facility Test

AUTHOR: John T. Dailey
DATE: 1977
PURPOSE: To evaluate levels of skill in the use of oral language for the language or dialect to which the individual has been exposed in his/her home environment
AGE RANGE: 3 to 15 years
WHO CAN ADMINISTER: Teachers or teacher aides who have studied the manual
TIME TO ADMINISTER: 10 minutes
DESCRIPTION: The author recommends using the Language Facility Test in bilingual educational, foreign language, and early education programs; in programs for the deaf and the physically or mentally handicapped; and in other programs for groups whose family language experiences have been atypical. The test is administered by showing the child 3 pictures and asking him/her to tell stories about the pictures. Twelve pictures are included in the test materials to make 3 alternate forms with 3 pictures each, plus 3 extra pictures to use as alternates. A tape recorder is considered desirable but not essential, since the examiner writes down the child's responses whether a recorder is used or not.

Two scoring methods are described in the 43-page manual. Using the first method, the examiner rates the child's responses on the basis of a 10-level scoring system. Brief definitions of the 10 levels are given on the test forms; the manual contains more detailed descriptions of the scoring criteria with examples of the 10 levels for each of the plates. Scores based on this method range from 0 ("No response—garbled speech, or only pointing at picture") to 9 ("A well-organized story with imagination and creativity. Need not be original. May use well-known fictional or historical characters.") Tables provided in the manual may be used to facilitate interpretation of scores. In addition to the original manual, there is a manual supplement, written in Spanish, which contains instructions for administration and scoring criteria.

A second scoring method is suggested as a way of obtaining diagnostic information regarding the individual's facility with standard English. By this method the rater refers to a table of 24 common deviations from standard English and tallies the number of deviations contained in the child's stories.

NORMS, RELIABILITY, VALIDITY: Manual provides detailed information

SOURCE: The Allington Corporation, 801 N. Pitt Street No. 707, Alexandria, Virginia 22314

APPROXIMATE COST: $33 for Manual, Test Plates, and 100 Answer Booklets

Language-Structured Auditory Retention Span Test (LARS)

AUTHOR: Luis Carlson

DATE: 1973

PURPOSE: To define and remediate or circumvent disabilities in language functioning

AGE RANGE: 3-7 through adult

WHO CAN ADMINISTER: Teachers, clinicians, and specialists who have studied the manual

TIME TO ADMINISTER: 20 minutes

DESCRIPTION: The instrument contains 58 items consisting of words, phrases, and sentences of increasing length and complexity. Some are of a nonsense type. The examiner reads the item in a monotone only once, and the child repeats it. The manual describes administration procedures, such as where to begin testing and when to stop. Method of scoring and criteria for Failure and Not Failure are listed. There are two forms, and it is suggested that the test be administered a second time if there are questions regarding results of the first testing. Instructions are given on the test form for converting raw scores to a mental age equivalent and verbal IQ.

NORMS, RELIABILITY, VALIDITY: None reported in manual

SOURCE: Academic Therapy Publications, 20 Commercial Boulevard, Novata, California 94947

APPROXIMATE COST: $9 for Manual and 25 Test Forms

Marysville Test of Language Dominance

AUTHOR: Eleanor Thonis
DATE: 1977
PURPOSE: To help schools make decisions about students who may need placement in special programs where strengths of the students form the basis for curriculum
AGE RANGE: Kindergarten to fifth grade
WHO CAN ADMINISTER: Teachers who have studied the directions. If the teacher is not bilingual, another person administers the instrument in the child's native language.
TIME TO ADMINISTER: Unspecified
DESCRIPTION: This experimental test is described as a structured interview in which the examiner attempts to determine the child's abilities by testing in English and again in Spanish. There are 10 items of increasing complexity under each of 5 categories, but preschoolers are given only the following 3 categories:

1. Listening (**Ex:** Child follows instructions to touch parts of the body, count, hop, etc.)
2. Speaking (**Ex:** Child answers questions about the family, child's hopes for the future, etc.)
3. Cultural (**Ex:** Examiner obtains information for these items from child's record and from questions such as "What language do you use when speaking to your brothers and sisters?")

There are separate sets of questions for English and for Spanish administration. The 8-page mimeographed manual amplifies directions for administering and scoring and discusses interpretation and various purposes and uses.
NORMS, RELIABILITY, VALIDITY: None reported in manual
SOURCES: Eleanor Thonis, Marysville Joint Unified School District, 1919 B Street, Marysville, California 94901
APPROXIMATE COST: Available from above source

Pictorial Test of Bilingualism and Language Dominance

AUTHORS: Darwin Nelson, Michael J. Fellner, and C. L. Norrell

DATE: 1975

PURPOSE: To measure language facility in English and Spanish

AGE RANGE: 4 to 8 years

WHO CAN ADMINISTER: Bilingual teachers who have studied the test manual or bilingual paraprofessionals who have been trained to administer the instrument

TIME TO ADMINISTER: 30 minutes

DESCRIPTION: The test is in 2 parts. Part I, Oral Vocabulary, consists of 40 picture cards designed to elicit particular vocabulary words. Part II, Oral Language Production, consists of a 2-card booklet and is recommended when additional information on bilingual language facility is required. In Part I, the child is asked to tell the examiner the name of each of the 40 pictures. After the child responds in one language he/she is asked to give the word in the other language. Scores are figured for English, Spanish, Bilingual, and Total Oral Vocabulary. These results convert into standard scores which are plotted on a diagnostic grid that places the child in 1 of 6 diagnostic categories: English Dominant, Spanish Dominant, Bilingual, Pseudobilingual, Language Deficient, and Suspected Mental Retardation or Language/Learning Disability.

In the first step of Part II, the child is asked to look at a picture and tell a story of what he/she sees. The answer is recorded verbatim and then the child is asked to tell the story in the other language. In the second step, the child is asked to respond to 2 questions about each of 2 pictures. The questions are asked in English and in Spanish and the child's English and Spanish responses are recorded. Responses are rated according to 4 levels that are described in the manual. The ratings provide additional information about the extent of the child's bilingualism and dominant oral language.

The 52-page manual includes suggested uses of the instrument and emphasizes the application of local norms. The instrument is considered to be a preliminary screening device to determine if additional evaluations are necessary.

NORMS, RELIABILITY, VALIDITY: Manual provides information

SOURCE: Stoelting Company, 1350 South Kostner Avenue, Chicago, Illinois 60623

APPROXIMATE COST: $22 for Manual, Oral Vocabulary Booklet, Language Production Booklet, 25 Answer Sheets

Preschool Language Scale (PLS)

AUTHORS: Ira L. Zimmerman, Violette G. Steiner, and Roberta L. Evatt

DATE: 1969

PURPOSE: To evaluate developmental progress, maturational lag, strengths and deficiencies in the language skills of young children, both normal and handicapped, which will aid in the development of language programs

AGE RANGE: 1-6 to 6-11 years

WHO CAN ADMINISTER: Child development specialists, such as psychologists, speech therapists, teachers, and administrators who have studied the manual

TIME TO ADMINISTER: 30 minutes

DESCRIPTION: The Preschool Language Scale consists of two sections, Auditory Comprehension and Verbal Ability. Each section contains 4 tests for each 6-month period, beginning with 1 year 6 months. Items are arranged in order of difficulty with each item counting as one and one-half months. A picture book is used for some of the items; other necessary materials can easily be provided by the examiner. The Auditory Comprehension section includes such items as knowing body parts, following directions, comparing size, distinguishing prepositions, grouping objects, recognizing colors, differentiating texture, and distinguishing weight differences. The Verbal Ability section includes such items as naming animals, pronouncing sounds correctly, naming opposites, repeating digits, repeating sentences, counting, conversing in sentences, giving name, etc.

The manual gives specific instructions for administering and scoring each item, rationale for use of the item, and references to authorities who have previously used the item at the particular age placement. Instructions are given for estimating an Auditory Comprehension Age and a Verbal Ability Age. A Language Age and a Language Quotient can then be calculated. A brief articulation test is provided at the end of the test booklet. The authors stress the importance of separating the auditory and verbal aspects of language skills since this allows the assessment of deficiencies that might otherwise be masked or overlooked.

NORMS, RELIABILITY, VALIDITY: None reported in the manual

SOURCE: Charles E. Merrill Publishing Company, 1300 Alum Creek Drive, Columbus, Ohio 43216

APPROXIMATE COST: $18 for Manual, Picture Book, and 10 Language Scales

Spanish/English Language Performance Screening (S/ELPS)

AUTHORS: Southwest Educational Development Laboratory, James H. Perry, Executive Director

DATE: 1976

PURPOSE: To determine a child's stronger or dominant language for intitial learning in a bilingual program

AGE RANGE: 4 and 5 year old children in day care and kindergarten

WHO CAN ADMINISTER: Bilingual persons, including teachers' aides, who are experienced in working with young children and who have studied the handbook and practiced administering the test

TIME TO ADMINISTER: 15 minutes

DESCRIPTION: The S/ELPS consists of a Spanish section, administered first, and an English section, administered second. The sections are parallel in content and sample 5 language activities: answering questions, naming objects, following directions, describing objects, and describing pictures. The child's responses are recorded verbatim on the 1-page form. The manual gives instructions for scoring, which is in terms of which language predominates in the child's responses. A Classification Table translates scores into categories of Spanish, Predominantly Spanish, Bilingual, Predominantly English, English, and Undetermined. Recommendations are given in the manual for designing educational programs for children in each category.

NORMS, RELIABILITY, VALIDITY: Manual provides detailed information

SOURCE: CTB/McGraw-Hill, Del Monte Research Park, Monterey, California 93940

APPROXIMATE COST: $45 for Manipulatives, Stimulus Pictures,

Handbooks, and 40 Record Forms in duplicate

Test for Auditory Comprehension of Language (TACL)

AUTHOR: Elizabeth Carrow-Woolfolk
DATE: 1973
PURPOSE: To measure a child's auditory comprehension of language structure
AGE RANGE: 3 to 6 years
WHO CAN ADMINISTER: Persons who hold a bachelor's degree in education, psychology, or sociology and have had significant testing experience
TIME TO ADMINISTER: 30 minutes
DESCRIPTION: The TACL utilizes a series of 101 three-picture plates; the child responds to the examiner's statement by pointing to one of the three pictures (**Ex:** "Find the car that is on the street"). Instructions in the manual are provided in both English and Spanish. The test form itself shows opposite each item the age at which 75 percent and 90 percent of children pass. Total raw scores may be converted to age-score equivalents and percentile ranks. A form for analysis of items into vocabulary, morphology, and syntax is provided on the last page of the test form.
NORMS, RELIABILITY, VALIDITY: Manual provides information
SOURCE: Teaching Resources Corporation, 50 Pond Park Road, Hingham, Massachusetts 02043
APPROXIMATE COST: $40 for Manual, Book of Plates, and 25 Scoring/Analysis Forms in either English or Spanish

Tests of General Ability: Inter-American Series

AUTHOR: Herschel T. Manul
DATE: 1972
PURPOSE: To provide a test of the ability to do academic work in general, with parallel English and Spanish editions
AGE RANGE: 4 to 5 years
WHO CAN ADMINISTER: Teachers who have studied the test manual and who are fluent in the language in which the test is

administered

TIME TO ADMINISTER: 20 to 25 minutes for each of two sessions of general ability to do academic work. These are provided for different grade levels and are available in an English version and a Spanish version. The Preschool Level contains 80 items. For each item, the examiner presents a card containing 3 to 5 drawings and tells the child what to do (**Ex:** "Find the house which has only *two windows*.") There are 4 types of exercises: Oral Vocabulary, Number, Association, and Classification. These yield a Verbal-Numerical Score based on 40 items, a Nonverbal Score based on 40 items, and a Total Score. The author recommends use of local norms in interpretation. The child can be tested in his/her native language of either English or Spanish and scores can be compared with classmates, or the child can be tested in both languages in order to compare his/her abilities in the two languages.

NORMS, RELIABILITY, VALIDITY: None available

SOURCE: Guidance Testing Associates of St. Mary's University, One Camino Santa Maria, San Antonio, Texas 78284

APPROXIMATE COST: $8 for Stimulus Cards, Directions for Administration, and 25 Answer Sheets

Test of Language Development (TOLD)

AUTHORS: Phyllis L. Newcomer and Donald D. Hammill

DATE: 1977

PURPOSE: To measure children's language competencies, strengths, and weaknesses

AGE RANGE: 4 to 6 years

WHO CAN ADMINISTER Teachers, counselors, psychologists, language therapists, or other professionals who have studied the manual

TIME TO ADMINISTER: Unspecified

DESCRIPTION: The TOLD consists of 70 items divided unevenly among 7 subtests:

1. Picture Vocabulary (**Ex:** Child points to 1 of 4 pictures when examiner says the name)
2. Oral Vocabulary (**Ex:** Child gives the meaning of a word)
3. Grammatic Understanding (**Ex:** Child points to 1 of 3 pictures that illustrates a sentence the examiner says)

4. Sentence Imitation (**Ex:** Child repeats sentences after examiner)
5. Grammatic Completion (**Ex:** Child supplies missing word in a sentence)
6. Word Discrimination (**Ex:** Child says whether 2 words pronounced by examiner are the same or different)
7. Word Articulation (**Ex:** Child says word illustrated by a picture or repeats word pronounced by examiner)

Testing on any subtest is usually discontinued after 5 consecutive failures. Raw scores are translated to a Language Age, a Language Quotient, and a Scaled Score, which are shown on a summary sheet and on a profile chart on the front of the answer booklet. The author emphasizes that the test does not provide a basis for planning instructional programs but does identify children who need further diagnostic and remedial attention.

NORMS, RELIABILITY, VALIDITY: Information available
SOURCE: PRO-ED, 333 Perry Brooks Building, Austin, Texas 78701
APPROXIMATE COST: $53 for kit that includes Test Manual, Statistical Manual, 25 Answer Sheets, and Picture Book

Vane Evaluation of Language Scale (VANE-L)

AUTHOR: Julia R. Vane
DATE: 1975
PURPOSE: To measure language acquisition in order to determine which children will need further help
AGE RANGE: 2-6 to 6 years
WHO CAN ADMINISTER: Teachers who have studied the manual or paraprofessionals who have been trained to administer the scale
TIME TO ADMINISTER: 10 minutes
DESCRIPTION: The scale consists primarily of two parts: Receptive Language and Expressive Language. The Receptive Language section taps knowledge of body parts, simple directions, and basic language concepts. Responses do not depend on verbal replies but on pointing (**Ex:** "Point to your knee") or showing (**Ex:** "Show me the bottle farthest from you"). A response to an item may be scored in several ways; specific in-

structions are given for doing this. The Expressive Language section measures the child's ability to express himself verbally by answering questions, repeating sentences, defining words, etc. In addition to the two main sections, there is a 2-item measure of Memory or Attention. There are also 8 items on the scale where the examiner notes which hand the child uses, and this helps determine whether or not dominance has been established.

Scores for the Receptive, Expressive, and Memory-Attention measures are converted to percentiles by age. The manual includes a form that may be used to report results to parents in order to encourage home participation with the child. The 30-page manual also includes sections on use of the scale as an individual diagnostic instrument, as an aid to classroom instruction, and as a research instrument.

NORMS, RELIABILITY, VALIDITY: Manual provides detailed information

SOURCE: Clinical Psychology Publishing Co., Inc., 4 Conant Square, Brandon, Vermont 04733

APPROXIMATE COST: $15 for Test Kit, Manual, and 40 Record Sheets

Verbal Language Development Scale

AUTHORS: Merline J. Mecham

DATE: 1958

PURPOSE: To provide an extension of the communication portion of the Vineland Social Maturity Scale

AGE RANGE: 1 month to 16 years

WHO CAN ADMINISTER: Teachers, clinicians, specialists, and trained paraprofessionals who have studied the manual and the book *Measurement of Social Competence* (interpretation should be done by clinicians, school psychologists, and other testing specialists)

TIME TO ADMINISTER: 15 to 30 minutes

DESCRIPTION: As with the Vineland Social Maturity Scale, an interviewer obtains information from an informant who knows the subject intimately. The 50 items in the Scale are classified under 9 age levels. There are 3 to 10 items under each age level, with the lower age levels containing more items. (Examples at the 3 to 4 year level are "Relates experiences" and "Says at least one nursery rhyme.") Each item is designated as pertaining to listening, speaking, reading, or writing. The manual gives instructions for scoring and gives a definition of each item. Total score is translated to a Language Age Equivalent by reference to a table in the manual.

NORMS, RELIABILITY, VALIDITY: Manual provides information
SOURCE: American Guidance Service, Inc., Publishers' Building, Circle Pines, Minnesota 55014
APPROXIMATE COST: $4 for Manual and 25 Score Sheets

Vocabulary Comprehension Scale

AUTHOR: Tina E. Bangs
DATE: 1975
PURPOSE: To determine a child's vocabulary functioning level
AGE RANGE: 2 to 6 years
WHO CAN ADMINISTER: Clinicians, or teachers who have attended a workshop on administration of the instrument
TIME TO ADMINISTER: 20 minutes
DESCRIPTION: The Scale provides information about a child's knowledge of pronouns and words of position, quality, quantity, and size. There are 61 key words included in separate sentences in which the examiner asks the child to carry out a specific activity. Toys are provided for these game-style activities, which are clustered under the following headings:

1. Garage (**Ex:** "Push the car backward.")
2. Tea Party (**Ex:** "He wants a napkin.")
3. Buttons (**Ex:** "Which box has less buttons?")
4. Miscellaneous (**Ex:** "Give me the soft one.")

Developmental norms are provided for each test item and scores may be translated to age levels. A summary sheet classifies word knowledge according to the language concept being tested. The manual includes suggestions to teachers and parents for teaching unfamiliar words and concepts.

NORMS, RELIABILITY, VALIDITY: Manual provides information
SOURCE: Teaching Resources Corporation, 100 Boylston Street,
Boston, Massachusetts 02116
APPROXIMATE COST: $40 for Manual, 25 Scoring Forms, and
Test Materials

MOTOR SKILLS

Bruininks-Oseretsky Test of Motor Proficiency

AUTHOR: Robert H. Bruininks
DATE: 1977
PURPOSE: To assess motor development
AGE RANGE: 4-6 to 14-6 years
WHO CAN ADMINISTER: Teachers who have attended a workshop on administration of this instrument
TIME TO ADMINISTER: Short Form — 20 minutes; Complete Battery — 60 minutes
DESCRIPTION The Complete Battery of 46 items provides a broad measure of gross and fine motor skills. The Short Form is composed of 14 of the items and is used for screening purposes. The Complete Battery yields scores on Gross Motor Composite (ability to use the large muscles of the shoulders, trunk, and legs); Fine Motor Composite (ability to use the small muscles of the fingers, hand, and forearm); and a Battery Composite (general motor development). The Short Form provides a single score comparable to the Battery Composite score. The manual includes illustrations to simplify test administration and scoring. Age equivalents are provided for each subtest.
NORMS, RELIABILITY, VALIDITY: Manual provides detailed information
SOURCE: American Guidance Service, Circle Pines, Minnesota 55014
APPROXIMATE COST: $105 for testing equipment, the Manual, 25 Individual Record Forms of the Complete Battery, a sample of the Short Form, 25 Student Booklets

Movement Skills Survey (MMS)

AUTHORS: R. E. Orpet and T. L. Heustis
DATE: 1971

PURPOSE: To evaluate selected aspects of a child's motor development in order to individualize movement education activities and organize the movement education curriculum

AGE RANGE: 3 to 7 years

WHO CAN ADMINISTER: Teachers, movement education supervisors, school psychologists and other professional school personnel

TIME TO ADMINISTER: Unspecified (observation checklist)

DESCRIPTION: The items in the MSS are grouped under 8 areas: Coordination and Rhythm, Agility, Flexibility, Strength, Speed, Balance, Endurance, and Body Awareness. Each item is defined and illustrative activities are listed. For example, "Agility" is defined as "The ability to initiate movement, change direction, or otherwise adjust position speedily." Illustrative activities for this particular item are dodgeball, shuttle runs, and sitting-to-standing exercises. Rating is on a 5-point scale ranging from Severely Impaired to Excellent. It is recommended that children with low ratings receive specific training in the area involved. The 1-page survey sheet, which also contains instructions for administration, includes coded numbers for suggested training activities, which are keyed to the Frostig-Maslow Move-Grow-Learn Program.

NORMS, RELIABILITY, VALIDITY: None available

SOURCE: Follett Publishing Company, 1010 West Washington Boulevard, Chicago, Illinois 60607

APPROXIMATE COST: $5 for pad of 100 sheets

Test of Motor Impairment

AUTHORS: D. H. Stott, F. A. Moyes, and S. E. Henderson

DATE: 1972

PURPOSE: To measure motor impairment as an indicator of neural dysfunction

AGE RANGE: 5 to 14 years

WHO CAN ADMINISTER: Clinicians, specialists, teachers who have attended a workshop or studied the manual, paraprofessionals trained to administer this instrument

TIME TO ADMINISTER: 20 minutes

DESCRIPTION: The test consists of 45 items based on the

Oseretsky Test of Motor Ability. There are 5 items for each of 9 age levels, beginning with age 4 and under and continuing to age 13 and over. Categories of motor function tested are:

1. Control and balance of the body while immobile
2. Control and coordination of the upper limbs
3. Control and coordination of the whole body while in motion
4. Manual dexterity with the emphasis on speed
5. Tasks which emphasize simultaneous movement and precision

Tasks vary according to age of the child. Instructions for administration and scoring are outlined in the manual according to the standard procedure, a shortened procedure, and a clinical procedure.

NORMS, RELIABILITY, VALIDITY: Manual provides information
SOURCE: Brook Educational Publishing Ltd., P. O. Box 1171, Guelph, Ontario NIH 6N3 Canada
APPROXIMATE COST: Available from above source

READINESS

ABC Inventory

AUTHORS: Normand Adair and George Blesch
DATE: 1965
PURPOSE: To identify children who are not mature enough for a standard school program
AGE RANGE: 3-6 to 6-6 years
WHO CAN ADMINISTER: Teachers or other school examiners who have studied manual
TIME TO ADMINISTER: 10 to 15 minutes
DESCRIPTION: The inventory has 4 sections; test items are placed according to difficulty within each section. The 4 sections require the child to draw a man, answer questions about the characteristics of objects (**Ex:** "Tell me the color of grass"); answer question about general topics (**Ex:** "What is ice when it melts?"); and complete some simple tasks involving numbers and shapes (**Ex:** "Copy a square"). Administration procedures and scoring criteria are described in detail.
NORMS, RELIABILITY, VALIDITY: Manual provides information
SOURCE: Educational Studies and Development, 1357 Forest Park Road, Muskegon, Michigan 49441
APPROXIMATE COST: $5 for Manual and 50 Inventories

Academic Readiness Scale

AUTHOR: Harold F. Burks
DATE: 1968
PURPOSE: To assess academic readiness in a way that allows a report of academic and personality status, identifies slow maturing or otherwise handicapped children, and enables the teacher to conduct a structured interview with parents
AGE RANGE: End of kindergarten or beginning of first grade
WHO CAN ADMINISTER: Teachers who have studied the manual

TIME TO ADMINISTER: Unspecified (rating scale and parent interview)

DESCRIPTION: The teacher rates each of 14 characteristics on a 5-point horizontal line. The checkmarks can then be joined to form a profile. Items cover the following areas of functioning: motor, perceptual-motor, persistence, memory, attention, number recognition, counting, word recognition, vocabulary, interest in curriculum, social, human, and emotional. As an example, the choices for the item on word recognition are: "cannot recognize any letters, knows some letters, can recognize first name, can recognize full name, can recognize several words." The final page of the 4-page form includes a list of questions the teacher should consider if the child is a candidate for retention or special placement. There is also a list of questions for the teacher to use in an interview with parents. The questions concern the parents' perceptions of the child's social, emotional, physical, and intellectual development with specific items listed under each of these.

NORMS, RELIABILITY, VALIDITY: Manual provides information

SOURCE: Arden Press, 8331 Alvarado Drive, Huntington Beach, California 92646

APPROXIMATE COST: $8 for Manual and 25 Tests

Anton Brenner Developmental Gestalt
Test of School Readiness (BGT)

AUTHOR: Anton Brenner

DATE: 1964

PURPOSE: To assess school readiness

AGE RANGE: 5 to 6 years

WHO CAN ADMINISTER: Teacher, examiner, or clinician who has studied the manual

TIME TO ADMINISTER: 3 to 10 minutes

DESCRIPTION: The main section of the BGT consists of 5 subtests, all of a numeric-perceptual nature: Number Producing (**Ex:** Child hands examiner varying numbers of blocks on request); Number Recognition (**Ex:** Child names number of dots in each of 10 groups of dots); Ten Dot Gestalt (**Ex:** Child copies a 10-dot figure); Sentence Gestalt (**Ex:** Child copies a printed sentence); and Draw-a-Man (**Ex:** Child draws a picture of a man). Instructions and illustrations for scoring are included in the manual; for example, the drawing of a man is scored according to 10 criteria. The total score for the 5 subtests is translated to a School Readiness Level (low, average, or high) based on chronological age of the child.

The examiner also rates the child on 2 Readiness Rating Scales based on observations made before, during, and immediately after testing. The Achievement-Ability Scale consists of 8 items (**Ex:** "Gives up easily," "Makes reasonable efforts," or is "Persistent and absorbed"). The Social-Emotional Behavior Scale also has 8 items (**Ex:** "Lacks self-confidence," "Is confident," or has a "High degree of self-confidence"). The total score for each of these 2 areas is converted to categories of Inadequate, Fair, Average, Good, or Excellent. The author discusses rationale for the BGT in terms of belief that perceptual-conceptual development is a principal factor in personality development, learning, and readiness for school.

NORMS, RELIABILITY, VALIDITY: Manual provides information
SOURCE: Western Psychological Services, 12031 Wilshire Boulevard, Los Angeles, California 90025
APPROXIMATE COST: $15 for test materials, Manual, and 25 Protocol Booklets

Basic School Skills Inventory (BSSI)

AUTHORS: Libby Goodman and Donald Hammill
DATE: 1975
PURPOSE: To evaluate school readiness in terms of skills actually required for success and to provide information that enables teachers to make instructional decisions about individual children
AGE RANGE: 4 to 7 years
WHO CAN ADMINISTER: Classroom teachers and their aides, diagnostic teachers, and other school personnel who have studied the manual and who see the child on a continuing basis
TIME TO ADMINISTER: Unspecified (checklist)
DESCRIPTION: To be completed within a time span of 1 week, the BSSI is an 84-item inventory of 7 areas of school performance. It is based on teachers' judgments (**Ex:** "Can the child

toilet himself properly without assistance?") and descriptions of desirable school performance (**Ex:** "Can the child wait his turn?") and is both norm-referenced and criterion-referenced. The pupil record sheet may be filled out by the teacher either at home or at school, with only the doubtful items being assessed directly at school. The 7 areas inventoried by the checklist are as follows: Basic Information, Self-Help, Handwriting, Oral Communication, Reading Readiness, Number Readiness, and Classroom Behavior. A 64-page manual includes the inventory, scoring tables, and directions for using the scale, as well as background and research data. Materials that are not readily available in the classroom are provided with the inventory in the form of 4 by 6 inch cards, one set each for number readiness, oral communication, reading readiness, and basic information.

NORMS, RELIABILITY, VALIDITY: Manual provides information
SOURCE: PRO-ED, 333 Perry Brooks Building, Austin, Texas 78701
APPROXIMATE COST: $20 for testing cards, Manual, and 30 Pupil Record Sheets

Boehm Test of Basic Concepts

AUTHOR: Ann E. Boehm
Date: 1971
PURPOSE: To measure childrens's mastery of concepts considered necessary for achievement in the first years of school
AGE RANGE: Preschool through second grade
WHO CAN ADMINISTER: Teachers who have studied the manual
TIME TO ADMINISTER: The test consists of 2 booklets, each having 3 sample items followed by 25 test items. Each item consists of a set of pictures about which statements are read aloud to the child by the examiner. The statements briefly describe the pictures and the child is asked to point to or mark with a crayon the picture that illustrates the concept being tested (**Ex:** "Look at the ducks in the water. Mark the duck that is *last*.") Some of the concepts are: different, middle, below, more, top, and last. Scores are transferred to a class record form that provides a summary of individual and class responses to

each item as well as total scores and percentile ranks for each child. This test may also be administered in small groups to children in K-2nd grade. Two forms of the test are available.

NORMS, RELIABILITY, VALIDITY: Manual provides detailed information

SOURCE: The Psychological Corporation, 757 Third Avenue, New York, New York 10017

APPROXIMATE COST: $8 for 30 Test Booklets (Form A or B), Manual, Class Record, Key

A Checklist for the Evaluation of Reading Readiness

AUTHOR: Joseph Sanacore
DATE: 1973
PURPOSE: To assess the child's readiness to begin formal reading instruction
AGE RANGE: 4 to 6 years
WHO CAN ADMINISTER: Teachers who have read the manual
TIME TO ADMINISTER: Checklist reflecting a number of informal observations made during the school year
DESCRIPTION: The classroom teacher responds Yes or No to 70 questions in 7 areas: auditory discrimination, visual discrimination, left to right orientation, oral language development, concept development, social and emotional development, and motor coordination. The author suggests that before making the final decision concerning a child's readiness for formal reading instruction the teacher consider information compiled from the following sources: the checklist, informal and standardized reading readiness tests, mental ability tests, anecdotal records, and conferences with parents.
NORMS, RELIABILITY, VALIDITY: None available
SOURCE: Joseph Sanacore, Hauppauge Public Schools, 600 Town Line Road, Hauppauge, New York 11787
APPROXIMATE COST: Available from above source upon request

Comprehensive Mathematics Inventory

AUTHORS: Robert E. Rea and Robert E. Keys
DATE: 1970

PURPOSE: To measure basic mathematic knowledge
AGE RANGE: Entering kindergarten
WHO CAN ADMINISTER: Teachers and other school personnel who have been trained to administer the instrument
TIME TO ADMINISTER: 35 to 40 minutes, divided into two sessions
DESCRIPTION: This Inventory contains 200 items divided into 7 categories:

1. Number (**Ex:** Child indicates from picture cards which group contains more objects)
2. Money (**Ex:** Child names coins and tells which will buy the most)
3. Measurement (**Ex:** Child indicates knowledge of "hotter" and "colder" as shown on an imitation thermometer)
4. Pattern Identification (**Ex:** Child completes a color pattern)
5. Recall (**Ex:** Child repeats pencil taps)
6. Vocabulary (**Ex:** Child indicates knowledge of such words as "over," "behind," "in front of")
7. Geometry (**Ex:** Child places shapes in formboards)

Testing materials may be assembled by the examiner. A test administration booklet includes instructions for administering and scoring. Results are to be used by teachers to assist in the development of programs and materials for use in early mathematics instruction.
NORMS, RELIABILITY, VALIDITY: Information available
SOURCE: NAPS document No. 00613, ASIS National Auxiliary Publication Service, CCM Information Sciences, Inc., 440 Park Avenue South, New York, New York 10016
APPROXIMATE COST: Available from above source

Cooperative Preschool Inventory: Revised Edition

AUTHOR: Bettye M. Caldwell
DATE: 1970
PURPOSE: To measure achievement in areas regarded as necessary for success in school
AGE RANGE: 3 to 6 years
WHO CAN ADMINISTER: Teachers who have studied the test

manual

TIME TO ADMINISTER: 15 minutes

DESCRIPTION: The Inventory contains 64 items that elicit information in the areas of personal and social responsiveness, associative vocabulary, and numerical and sensory concepts. Examples of items are: "What is your name?" "When do we eat breakfast?" "Which way does an elevator go?". Answers are scored as Correct or Incorrect; answers are shown below each question in the administrator's manual. The total score on the Inventory may be translated to a percentile ranking by age level. The Inventory originally was developed in 1965 for use with disadvantaged children at the time of initiation of Project Head Start. The manual includes a discussion of the history, purpose, and standardization of the instrument.

NORMS, RELIABILITY, VALIDITY: Manual provides information

SOURCE: Addison-Wesley Testing Service, One South Street, Reading, Massachusetts 01867

APPROXIMATE COST: $6 for Directions for Administering and Scoring, 20 Answer Recording Leaflets, and Handbook

Daberon: A Screening Device for School Readiness

AUTHORS: Virginia A. Danzer, Theresa M. Lyons, and Mary Frances Gerber

DATE: 1972

PURPOSE: To predict readiness for school activities and to establish the baseline of a continuing record of educational progress

AGE RANGE: 4 through 6 years

WHO CAN ADMINISTER: Teachers or teacher aides who have been trained to administer the test

TIME TO ADMINISTER: 20 minutes

DESCRIPTION: A large portion of the Daberon is devoted to the assessment of language skills. A total of 124 items are included in the test; the age and ability level of the child determine which items are used. Areas surveyed are knowledge of body parts, color and number concepts, functional use of prepositions, plurals, ability to follow directions, general knowledge, visual perception, gross motor development, and ability to categorize. A high percentage of accurate responses on the Daberon is considered by the authors to indicate school readiness, while inaccurate responses may indicate future problem areas or a need for further diagnosis or specific teaching. A 27-page manual gives instructions for administering and scoring and lists suggested diagnostic instruments and remedial materials.

NORMS, RELIABILITY, VALIDITY: None available
SOURCE: Daberon Research, 4202 SW 44th Avenue, Portland, Oregon 97221
APPROXIMATE COST: $12 for Picture Cards, Manual, and 50 Screen Forms

Developmental Tasks for Kindergarten Readiness (DTKR)

AUTHOR: Walter J. Lesiak
DATE: 1978
PURPOSE: To determine kindergarten readiness
AGE RANGE: 4-6 to 6-2 years
WHO CAN ADMINISTER: School psychologists, teachers, other school personnel, or trained paraprofessionals, who have studied the manual
TIME TO ADMINISTER: 20 to 30 minutes
DESCRIPTION: This instrument is administered prior to a child's entrance into kindergarten and provides school personnel with objective data about a child's skills and abilities as they relate to successful performance in kindergarten. The DTKR consists of 12 subtests in these 4 areas: oral language (auditory sequencing, auditory association); visual motor (visual discrimination, visual memory, visual motor, name printing); cognitive (body concepts, color naming, number knowledge, alphabet knowledge, relational concepts); social development (social interaction). The test yields 12 subtest scores and a profile of strengths and weaknesses that can be used by school personnel to plan remedial activities if necessary.

NORMS, RELIABILITY, VALIDITY: Manual provides detailed information
SOURCE: Clinical Psychology Publishing Company, Inc., 4 Conant Square, Brandon, Vermont 05733
APPROXIMATE COST: Available from above source

Early Detection Inventory (EDI)

AUTHORS: F. E. McGahan and Carolyn McGahan
DATE: 1975
PURPOSE: To evaluate a child's readiness for a successful school experience
AGE RANGE: 3-6 to 7-6 years
WHO CAN ADMINISTER: Clinicians or specialists, teachers who have attended a workshop or who have studied the test manual, paraprofessionals who have been trained to administer the inventory (to be interpreted by clinicians, school psychologists, or other testing specialists)
TIME TO ADMINISTER: 30 minutes
DESCRIPTION: The EDI elicits information in the following areas:

1. Social-Emotional (a checklist for behavior observed during the testing procedure, such as "Pleasant; smiling" or "Disagreeable; frowning")
2. School Readiness (items concerning child's verbal self-awareness, concept development, awareness of left and right, awareness of body image)
3. Motor Performance (items pertaining to gross motor coordination, fine motor coordination, hand preference, and eye preference)
4. Physical Information (brief ratings and comments concerning eye, dental, audiometric, and speech problems as ascertained by the school nurse or other specialists)
5. Personal History (21 questions concerning family and social history and 17 questions concerning prenatal, birth, child, and family medical history)

General age expectancies are discussed in the manual for some of the fine-motor and gross-motor tasks but emphasis is on the examiner's careful observation and judgment. Ratings on most of the tasks are according to whether performance is Successful, Partial, or Unsuccessful; or in some cases whether Good, Fair, or Poor. An Overall Readiness Number is based on the subscale ratings.

A preschool clinic involving a station approach is recommended for administration of the 13-page Inventory, and instructions for setting up such a clinic are given in the manual. Findings are to be interpreted to parents so they can take steps to help remedy learning difficulties before the child enters school. Materials for parents and teachers concerning the learning disabled child are available.

NORMS, RELIABILITY, VALIDITY: None reported in manual
SOURCE: N.E.T. Educational Service Center, Inc., 3065 Clark Lane, Paris, Texas 75460
APPROXIMATE COST: $17 for Manual and 25 Inventory Forms

Early School Inventory

AUTHORS: Joanne R. Nurss and Mary E. McGauvran
DATE: 1976
PURPOSE: To obtain relevant information about child development in several areas important for early school progress
AGE RANGE: Kindergarten or first grade
WHO CAN ADMINISTER: Teachers who have had an opportunity to observe pupils for a reasonable length of time
TIME TO ADMINISTER: Unspecified (checklist)
DESCRIPTION: This teacher's checklist consists of 82 items, which are divided into 5 sections. Each section contains several subheadings with a number of items under each.

1. Physical Development (Large Muscle Development, Fine Muscle Development, Sensory Development, General Condition of Health)
2. Language Development (Articulation and Fluency, Vocabulary, Use of Language Skills)
3. Cognitive Development (Information, Awareness of Details, Memory, Temporal and Spatial Concepts)
4. Social-Emotional Development (Intrapersonal Skills and Interpersonal Skills)
5. Parent Interview (Nine questions to parents, such as whether the child washes own face and hand)

The 6-page Inventory Form begins with a discussion of purposes, uses, and directions for completing the Inventory. Each section begins with a brief discussion of rationale for type of items included. Scoring is in terms of Yes, No, and ? (uncertain). If necessary, a situation may be arranged to elicit responses.

This Inventory was designed to supplement the results of standardized tests such as the Metropolitan Readiness Tests, and the authors suggest the information should be considered in relation to such measures. A handbook of skill development activities is available.

NORMS, RELIABILITY, VALIDITY: None reported in Inventory Booklet

SOURCE: The Psychological Corporation, 757 Third Avenue, New York, New York 10017

APPROXIMATE COST: $8 for 35 Early School Inventory Forms

Inventory of Readiness Skills

AUTHORS: Jack Shelquist, Barbara Breeze, and Bette Jacquot
DATE: 1973
PURPOSE: To assist the teacher in making a diagnostic assessment of the child's understanding of selected fundamental skills before a formalized instructional program is begun
AGE RANGE: Preschool through first grade
WHO CAN ADMINISTER: Teachers and remedial specialists who have studied the manual
TIME TO ADMINISTER: 20 minutes
DESCRIPTION: The manual provides a definition, rationale, procedure, and scoring instructions for the following 8 tests that comprise the inventory:

1. Auditory Memory Sequential (**Ex:** Child repeats words after examiner)
2. Word Discrimination (**Ex:** Child says whether the words he hears are alike or different)
3. Body Awareness (**Ex:** Child identifies body parts)
4. Locational and Directional Concepts (**Ex:** Child follows instructions such as "Make a mark outside the circle")
5. Color Discrimination (**Ex:** Child follows instructions such as "Take your red crayon and make a red mark here")
6. Visual-Motor Coordination (**Ex:** Child follows instructions such as "Draw a line across the dots")
7. Visual Memory, Letter Perception (**Ex:** Child finds letter in

test booklet after seeing it on a card for 5 seconds)
8. Letter Names (**Ex:** Child identifies letters)

The scores are transferred to an individual profile sheet for each student. Instructions for interpreting the profile are in the manual. The manual also lists behavioral objectives for each of the tests in the inventory. A handbook for development of learning skills is available separately.

NORMS, RELIABILITY, VALIDITY: Manual provides information
SOURCE: Educational Programmers, Inc., P. O. Box 332, Roseburg, Oregon 97470
APPROXIMATE COST: $13 for Manual, 20 Tests, 1 set Visual Memory Cards, 1 Mask

Keymath Diagnostic Arithmetic Test

AUTHORS: Austin Connolly, William Nachtman, and E. Milo Pritchett
DATE: 1976
PURPOSE: To provide a diagnostic assessment of skill in arithmetic
AGE RANGE: Kindergarten through seventh grade
WHO CAN ADMINISTER: Teachers who have studied the manual and paraprofessionals who have been trained to administer the test
TIME TO ADMINISTER: 30 minutes
DESCRIPTION: An easel type book is provided to show testing material to the child and very little reading or writing is required. There are 14 subtests that cover 3 basic areas: Content, Operations, and Application. The Content area involves numeration, fractions, geometry, and symbols; the Operations area involves addition, subtraction, multiplication, division, mental computations, and numerical reasoning; and the Application area involves word problems, missing elements, money, measurement, and time. A basal level is established by 3 consecutive correct responses and a ceiling level by 3 consecutive errors. A system of recording responses on a horizontal line provides a final summary and profile. The test yields 4 levels of diagnostic information: total test performance, performance in

each area, subtest performance, and item performance. The 54-page manual includes a statement of the behavioral objective for each of the 196 items.

NORMS, RELIABILITY, VALIDITY: Manual provides information
SOURCE: American Guidance Service, Circle Pines, Minnesota 55014
APPROXIMATE COST: $28 for Test Items, 25 Diagnostic Record, and Manual in an Easel-Kit

Kraner Preschool Math Inventory (KPMI)

AUTHOR: Robert E. Kraner
DATE: 1976
PURPOSE: To analyze mathematical skills and concepts and to help teachers target instructional strategies and remediation programs on an individual basis
AGE RANGE: 3 to 6-6 years
WHO CAN ADMINISTER: Teachers who have studied the manual
TIME TO ADMINISTER: 45 to 75 minutes
DESCRIPTION: The KPMI is a criterion-referenced test which covers skills and concepts that are considered to be prerequisites to common first-grade academic requirements or, in the case of preschool children, appropriate to cognitive development. There are 7 categories in the Inventory: Counting, Cardinal Numbers, Quantities, Sequence, Position, Direction, and Geometry and Measurement. Three performance exercises are provided for each of 77 concepts.

A 21-item norm-referenced Math/Screen test accompanies the KPMI, to be administered at the end of kindergarten or at the beginning of first grade for the purpose of determining placement.

NORMS, RELIABILITY, VALIDITY: Manual provides information
SOURCE: Teaching Resources Corporation, 50 Pond Park Road, Hingham, Massachusetts 02043
APPROXIMATE COST: $50 for Manual, 25 Scoring Forms, Classroom Record Sheet, 5 Instructional Record Forms, and 25 Math/Screen Test Booklets

Maturity Level for School Entrance and Reading Readiness

AUTHOR: Katharine M. Banham

DATE: 1959

PURPOSE: To help identify children who are mature enough to enter first grade regardless of chronological age

AGE RANGE: Kindergarten through first grade

WHO CAN ADMINISTER: Teachers who have studied the manual

TIME TO ADMINISTER: 15 minutes

DESCRIPTION: This instrument consists of a checklist of 25 items. There are 5 items (**Ex:** "The child can hop on one foot") under each of the following headings: Bodily Coordination, Eye-Hand Coordination, Speech and Language Comprehension, Personal Independence, and Social Cooperation. Scoring criteria and instructions are given in the 6-page manual. Scores indicate various levels of readiness for school entrance and readiness for reading.

NORMS, RELIABILITY, VALIDITY: Manual provides information

SOURCE: American Guidance Service, Inc., Circle Pines, Minnesota 50014

APPROXIMATE COST: $5 for Manual and 50 Individual Check Lists

Readiness for Kindergarten: A Coloring Book for Parents

AUTHOR: James O. Massey

DATE: 1979

PURPOSE: To help parents determine how ready their child may be for kindergarten

AGE RANGE: Unspecified

WHO CAN ADMINISTER: Parents who have read the instructions

TIME TO ADMINISTER: Not specified (checklist)

DESCRIPTION: Using a coloring book format, this device enables parents to evaluate their preschool child's readiness in the areas of intellectual, physical, and social-emotional development. The coloring book (which does not require coloring) contains 58 3 by 4 inch drawings that depict and describe tasks that Most, Many, Half, Few, and Very Few children entering kindergarten can do. For example, "most" children entering kindergarten can "take care of toilet needs without help." The parents are instructed to check the "OK" box if their child can do the task readily, check the "?" box if their child can do the task only barely or occasionally, or check the "No" box if their child has not yet learned to do the task. The parents add up the items checked "OK" and compare the total to the totals given in the booklet that indicate readiness for kindergarten.

Because each item is classified as either "thinking," "moving," or "feeling," the parents can also evaluate their child's performance in each of these areas. Suggestions for helping children develop skills in the 3 areas are included in the booklet. All instructions for administering and interpreting are included in the 16-page booklet.

NORMS, RELIABILITY, VALIDITY: Information available
SOURCE: Consulting Psychologists Press, 577 College Avenue, Palo Alto, California 94306
APPROXIMATE COST: $25 for 25 Coloring Booklets

Riley Preschool Developmental Screening Inventory

AUTHOR: Clara M. D. Riley
DATE: 1969
PURPOSE: To give the teacher an indication of the child's present developmental age and self-concept
AGE RANGE: 3 to 5 years
WHO CAN ADMINISTER: Psychologists or counselors who have studied the manual, teachers who have received inservice training on how to administer
TIME TO ADMINISTER: 3 to 10 minutes
DESCRIPTION: The Inventory consists of 2 parts: Design Drawing and Make-A-Boy (Girl). In the first part, the child is instructed to copy the 5 geometric designs that are illustrated in the 4-page inventory booklet. The examiner assists the child by tracing the design with his/her finger and then having the child do the same. The child then is given 3 chances to draw each design. In the second part, the child is instructed to "make a boy (girl)" in the space provided in the inventory booklet. Scoring instructions are printed on the front page of the booklet. The 10-page manual provides more detailed information on how to score the designs and drawings, interpretation of scores and recommendations for retesting or referral. The author re-

commends that the inventory be administered either before or within two weeks of the beginning of the program in which the child is to be involved. The inventory may also be administered to small groups of 2 or 3 children as well as to an entire class.

NORMS, RELIABILITY, VALIDITY: Information available
SOURCE: Western Psychological Services, 12031 Wilshire Boulevard, Los Angeles, California 90025
APPROXIMATE COST: $9 for Manual and 25 Test Booklets

School Readiness Checklist — Ready or Not?

AUTHORS: John J. Austin and J. Clayton Lafferty
DATE: 1968
PURPOSE: To help parents evaluate a child's development and to provide a better basis for school cooperation
AGE RANGE: 5 to 6 years
WHO CAN ADMINISTER: Parents who have read the instructions
TIME TO ADMINISTER: 10 minutes (or at parent's convenience)
DESCRIPTION: The Checklist, which may be part of a school-sponsored program, consists of 43 items (**Ex:** "Can your child tie a knot?") that require a Yes-No response. The items are presented in groups divided into 7 areas: Growth and Age, General Activity Related to Growth, Practical Skills, Remembering, Understanding, General Knowledge, and Attitudes and Interests. A table at the end of the test booklet indicates the approximate state of readiness for school according to the total number of "yes" responses. The readiness level is shown in 5 classifications ranging from "readiness reasonably assured" to "readiness unlikely." After determining the child's level of readiness, the parent is encouraged to consult with school personnel regarding the child's checklist results and class placement. A 91-page handbook includes a discussion of the concept of readiness, a section on educational programs that emphasize readiness, and references. A Spanish edition is available.
NORMS, RELIABILITY, VALIDITY: Manual provides information
SOURCE: Research Concepts, 1368 East Airport Road, Muskegon, Michigan 49444

APPROXIMATE COST: $11 for Handbook and 50 Test Booklets

School Readiness Survey

AUTHORS: F. L. Jordan and James Massey
DATE: 1969
PURPOSE: To help professional personnel involve the parents of preschool children in evaluating their children's developmental level and in preparing them for kindergarten
AGE RANGE: 4 to 6 years
WHO CAN ADMINISTER Parents who have studied the manual
TIME TO ADMINISTER: 30 to 45 minutes (may be administered in 2 or more sessions)
DESCRIPTION: The School Readiness Survey consists of 146 items divided unevenly among 7 sections:

1. Number Concepts (**Ex:** Child counts from 3 to 9 boxes)
2. Discrimination of Form (**Ex:** Child puts mark on the picture or shape that is not like the others)
3. Color Naming (**Ex:** Child names the color of 7 colored circles)
4. Symbol Matching (**Ex:** Child draws line between pictures, letters, words and symbols that are the same)
5. Speaking Vocabulary (**Ex:** Parent points to a picture and asks child "What is this?")
6. Listening Vocabulary (**Ex:** Child is instructed to put a mark on the picture of the word the parent pronounces)
7. General Information (**Ex:** Child answers questions)

For each section the survey booklet provides suggestions for the parent to help children develop necessary skills. A general readiness checklist is also included but not scored. Parent responds "yes" or "no" to questions about the child (**Ex:** "Is your child aware of dangers such as electricity, traffic, high places, fire?"). Directions for administering and for scoring and interpreting the scores, in terms of school readiness, are included in the 28-page test booklet.

A 14-page manual is available for school personnel use. Authors suggest that schools distribute the survey to parents at the time of preregistration for kindergarten.

NORMS, RELIABILITY, VALIDITY: Manual provides information
SOURCE: Consulting Psychologists Press, 577 College Avenue, Palo Alto, California 94306
APPROXIMATE COST: $14 for 25 Test Booklets and Manual

SEARCH: A Scanning Instrument for the Identification of Potential Learning Disability

AUTHORS: Archie A. Silver and Rosa A. Hagin
DATE: 1976
PURPOSE: To identify children in need of clinical services and educational intervention to support and supplement classroom instruction
AGE RANGE: 5-3 to 6-8 years
WHO CAN ADMINISTER: School personnel who have been trained in a one day workshop
TIME TO ADMINISTER: 20 minutes
DESCRIPTION: SEARCH consists of 10 components described briefly below:

1. Discrimination (**Ex:** Child is given a card containing a simple design and is asked to find in a group of identical designs in various positions the one that exactly matches the card)
2. Recall (**Ex:** Child matches drawings from memory after brief observation)
3. Designs (**Ex:** Child copies geometric designs of increasing difficulty)
4. Rote Sequencing (**Ex:** Child answers such questions as, "What number comes after 6?")
5. Auditory Discrimination (**Ex:** Child indicates ability to distinguish similarities and differences in words by answering such questions as, "Is this a mar?" when handed a toy car)
6. Articulation (**Ex:** Child repeats words pronounced by the examiner)
7. Initials (**Ex:** Child writes the beginning letter of each of 10 children's names pronounced by the examiner)
8. Directionality (**Ex:** Child follows 10 instructions such as, "Hold the car behind you.")

9. Finger Schema (**Ex:** Child points to a finger or fingers touched by the examiner when the child's eyes are closed)
10. Pencil Grip (**Ex:** Child's pencil grip is rated by examiner)

Specific instructions are given for administration and scoring. A stanine profile of the 10 components is prepared. The 102-page manual includes a section on interpretation. For example, certain scores are considered to be indicative of probable reading readiness, developmental delay, or neurological impairment. The authors stress the importance of educational planning, and a teacher resource book that contains instructional material keyed to SEARCH is available. Testing and resource materials were developed at the New York University Medical Center.

NORMS, RELIABILITY, VALIDITY: Manual provides information
SOURCE: Walker Educational Book Corporation, 720 Fifth Avenue, New York, New York 10019
APPROXIMATE COST: $25 for SEARCH Kit which includes Manual and Record Forms; $25 for teacher resource book, TEACH

Test of Directional Skills

AUTHOR: Graham M. Sterritt
DATE: 1971
PURPOSE: To evaluate ability of left-right and top-to-bottom sentence tracking
AGE RANGE: 3 to 7 years
WHO CAN ADMINISTER: Teachers who have read instructions; paraprofessionals trained to administer the instrument
TIME TO ADMINISTER: 15 minutes
DESCRIPTION: The test consists of 12 questions that the examiner asks as he/she shows 12 cards to the child. Questions are of the following type: "Point to where the sentence begins"; "Use your finger to show how these sentences go from the beginning of the first sentence to the end of the last one". Score is based on number of correct responses.
NORMS, RELIABILITY, VALIDITY: Information available
SOURCE: Kinesthetic Teacher Corporation, 560 South Carona,

Denver, Colorado 80209
APPROXIMATE COST: $7 for Test Card Set and 25 Test Forms

Walker Readiness Test for Disadvantaged Preschool Children

AUTHOR: Wanda Walker
DATE: 1969
PURPOSE: To measure school readiness of disadvantaged preschool children
AGE RANGE: 4 to 6 years
WHO CAN ADMINISTER: Teachers who have studied the manual
TIME TO ADMINISTER: 10 minutes
DESCRIPTION: This test has 2 forms. Form A is to be administered early in the school year to identify weaknesses and to help set up individual remedial programs. Form B is to be administered during the final weeks of the school year to assess the efficiency of the program used and the progress of the child. The test consists of 50 pictorial items divided into 4 subtests:

1. Likenesses and Similarities (**Ex:** Examiner points to a picture on the left and says, "Show me the one [of 4 pictures] that looks just like this one.")
2. Differences (**Ex:** Examiner points to a group of 4 pictures and says, "Show me the one that does not look like the others.")
3. Numerical Analogies (**Ex:** Examiner points to the picture on the left and says, "Now, show me the one [of 4 pictures] over here that has the same number as this one.")
4. Missing Parts (**Ex:** Examiner points to the picture on the left and says, "Now point to the one [of 4 pictures] over here which belongs to this one.")

The pictures (line drawings) cover a wide variety of objects, designs, numbers, letters, words, etc. The examiner's wording for each part of the test is written in English, French, and Spanish and the child responds by pointing. A stencil is used to score the answer sheet. Total scores may be compared with means and percentiles by age.

Norms, Reliability, Validity: Information available

Source: Regional Office of Education, Bureau of Research, Kansas City, Missouri 66101; ERIC Document Reproduction Service, P. O. Box 190, Arlington, Virginia 22210; and Wanda Walker, Northwest Missouri State College, Marysville, Missouri 64468

Approximate Cost: Available from above sources

Category 6

SOCIOEMOTIONAL

A-M-L Behavior Rating Scale

AUTHOR: Phyllis P. Van Fleet
DATE: 1978
PURPOSE: To provide quick screening for school dysfunction
AGE RANGE: Preschool through high school
WHO CAN ADMINISTER: Teacher who has taught the student for at least 3 months and has read instructions
TIME TO ADMINISTER: Unspecified (rating scale)
DESCRIPTION: This 11-item scale contains 3 subscales: Aggression (5 items), Moodiness (5 items), and Learning Difficulty (1 item). The teacher checks behavior characteristics on a 5-point scale ranging from Seldom or Never to All of the Time. Examples of items used in each of the subscales are: "A — Gets into fights or quarrels with other pupils"; "M — Is unhappy or depressed"; and "L — Has difficulty learning".
NORMS, RELIABILITY, VALIDITY: Information available
SOURCE: Phyllis Van Fleet, Ph.D., 243 Asilomar Boulevard, Pacific Grove, California 93950
APPROXIMATE COST: Available from above source upon request (4 duplicated pages)

Animal Crackers: A Test of Motivation to Achieve

AUTHORS: Dorothy C. Adkins and Bonnie Ballif
DATE: 1975 (Revision of Gumpgoohies, 1970)
PURPOSE: To provide a measure of those aspects of achievement-oriented behavior that are not attributable to intellectual abilities
AGE RANGE: 3-6 to 8 years
WHO CAN ADMINISTER: Teachers who have studied the manual
TIME TO ADMINISTER: 20 to 45 minutes
DESCRIPTION: The test contains 60 two-choice items designed to

provide information on 5 variables regarded by the authors as essential components of achievement motivation. These components are school enjoyment, self-confidence, purposive behavior, instrumental activity, and self-evaluation. The administrator points to illustrations of pairs of identical animals and asks the child to indicate which one of the animals is like him in interests (**Ex:** "This rabbit likes to spend the day at school; this rabbit likes to stay at home. Which one is yours?"). The test is not recommended for use with bilingual children whose lack of facility in English would preclude valid testing. The manual contains instructions for both group and individual administration, but individual administration is preferred for preschoolers or very immature children. Test may be scored by hand or by machine.

NORMS, RELIABILITY, VALIDITY: Manual provides detailed information

SOURCE: CTB/McGraw-Hill, Del Monte Research Park, Monterey, California 93940

APPROXIMATE COST: $15 for Manual and 30 Test Booklets

Barber Scales of Self-Regard: Preschool Form

AUTHORS: Lucie W. Barber and the Research Staff of the Union College Character Research Project

DATE: 1975

PURPOSE: To help parents assess and teach positive self-regard

AGE RANGE: 2 to 5 years

WHO CAN ADMINISTER: Parents especially, but also teachers who have studied the manual and teacher aides who have been trained to administer the instrument

TIME TO ADMINISTER: 20 minutes for each of 7 scales

DESCRIPTION: This instrument consists of 7 separate scales, titled Purposeful Learning of Skills, Completing Tasks, Coping with Fears, Children's Responses to Requests, Dealing with Frustrations, Socially Acceptable Behavior, and Developing Imagination in Play. Each scale is printed on a triplefold sheet, which describes 5 stages toward the development of positive self-regard in that particular area. For each of the 5 stages described on the sheet, there are 4 examples given to help the rater determine which level is most typical of the child he or she is rating. For example, Stage 3 on the Coping with Fears scale is shown as follows:

CHILDREN ARE COPING WHEN GIVEN REASSU-RANCE

They respond to fears by trying to be brave but they seem to recognize their need for parental reassurance. They want their parents nearby when they are fearful.

One of the accompanying examples is, "She really enjoyed our trip to the game farm but never left our side as we walked around looking at the animals." A 16-page Guide for Parents provides suggestions for rating and developing positive self-regard and includes a parent worksheet for each of the scales. The 25-page Technical Manual describes research related to the development of the scales. According to the manual, educational materials geared to scale points for each of the Scales were being prepared.

NORMS, RELIABILITY, VALIDITY: None available

SOURE: Character Research Press, 207 State Street, Schenectady, New York 12305

APPROXIMATE COST: $12 for Parents' Packet and Technical Manual

Bristol Social-Adjustment Guides

AUTHORS: D. H. Scott and N. C. Marston

DATE: 1970

PURPOSE: To help in the detection of emotional instability

AGE RANGE: 5 to 16 years

WHO CAN ADMINISTER: Teachers or other adults who have read the instructions and have had contact with the child in school over a period of a month or more (to be interpreted by a clinician or specialist)

TIME TO ADMINISTER: 15 minutes

DESCRIPTION: The instrument contains 33 behavioral items, which are divided into 7 areas. The teacher evaluates the child's behavior, underlining one of several descriptive phrases (**Ex:** "avoids teacher but talks to other children"). The areas are Interaction with Teacher, School Work, Games and Play, Attitudes to Other Children, Personal Ways, Physique, and School Achievement. Templates are provided for scoring according to diagnostic categories that are discussed in the manual. Cut-off scores, for use in judging severity of maladjustment, are shown for 2 main scales (Under-Reaction and Over-Reaction) and for 5 core syndromes.

NORMS, RELIABILITY, VALIDITY: Manual provides detailed information

SOURCE: Educational and Industrial Testing Service, P. O. Box 7234, San Diego, California 92107

APPROXIMATE COST: $10 for Manual, Scoring Keys, and 25 Scales (separate scales for boys and girls)

Brown IDS Self-Concept Referents Test

AUTHOR: Burt Brown

DATE: 1966—1973

PURPOSE: To measure the self-concept of a young child

AGE RANGE: Preschool to kindergarten

WHO CAN ADMINISTER: Teachers and paraprofessionals who have been trained to administer the instrument

TIME TO ADMINISTER: 10 to 15 minutes

DESCRIPTION: Three versions of this test have been used in several large scale evaluations of early childhood programs. A Polaroid full-length picture of the child is taken at the beginning of the test session. Depending on which version of the test is used, 15 to 21 bipolar questions are presented to the child as he/she looks at the self picture. Some questions ask for self descriptions (**Ex:** "Is ——— happy or is he/she sad?"). Other questions ask about behaviors (**Ex:** "Does ——— like to play with other kids or doesn't he/she like to play with other kids?"). The longest version of the test also includes 5 teacher-referent items.

NORMS, RELIABILITY, VALIDITY: Information available

SOURCE: ERIC Document Reproduction Service, P. O. Box 190, Arlington, Virginia 22210 (16-item version); V. C. Shipman, Educational Testing Services, Princeton, New Jersey 08540 (15-item version); Stanford Research Institute, Menlo Park, California 94025 (21-item version)

APPROXIMATE COST: Available from above sources

Burks' Behavior Rating Scales: Preschool and Kindergarten

AUTHOR: Harold F. Burks
DATE: 1977
PURPOSE: To identify particular behavior problems and patterns of problems shown by children
AGE RANGE: 3 through 6 years
WHO CAN ADMINISTER: Parents, teachers who have observed the child on a day-to-day basis for at least 2 weeks, and clinicians (results are interpreted by a clinician or other testing specialist)
TIME TO ADMINISTER: Unspecified (rating scale)
DESCRIPTION: The rater uses a scale of 1 (You have not noticed the behavior at all) to 5 (You have noticed the behavior to a very large degree) to respond to 105 items. Each of the items describes a behavior that is infrequently observed among normal children (**Ex:** "Avoids physical contact in play"). Scores are derived for 18 categories of behavior:

1. Excessive self blame
2. Excessive anxiety
3. Excessive withdrawal
4. Excessive dependency
5. Poor ego strength
6. Poor physical strength
7. Poor coordination
8. Poor intellectuality
9. Poor attention
10. Poor impulse control
11. Poor reality contact
12. Poor sense of identity
13. Excessive suffering
14. Poor anger control
15. Excessive sense of persecution
16. Excessive aggressiveness
17. Excessive resistance
18. Poor social conformity

Category scores are plotted on a profile sheet, which classifies each of the 18 scores as Not Significant, Significant, or Very Significant.

Approximately half of the 35-page manual is devoted to description of the 18 categories, with suggested intervention approaches. The remainder of the manual contains tables and discussion of the development and standardization of the scale.
NORMS, RELIABILITY, VALIDITY: Manual provides information
SOURCE: Arden Press, Box 844, Huntington Beach, California 92648

APPROXIMATE COST: $14 for Manual, 25 Booklets, and 25 Profile Sheets

California Preschool Social Competency Scale

AUTHORS: Samuel Levine, Freeman F. Elzey, and Mary Lewis
DATE: 1969
PURPOSE: To evaluate social competence
AGE RANGE: 2-6 through 5-6 years
WHO CAN ADMINISTER: Teacher who has read the manual and has had sufficient opportunity to observe the child's interaction with other children
TIME TO ADMINISTER: Unspecified (rating scale)
DESCRIPTION: The teacher rates the child in 30 areas of social functioning, such as communicating wants, response to unfamiliar adults, remembering instructions, and accepting limits. Rating is accomplished by selecting, for each of the 30 items, 1 of 4 descriptive phrases or statements that best describes the typical response or level of competence. For example, on the item Playing with Others, the teacher selects one of the following: "(1) He usually plays by himself; (2) He plays with others but limits play to one or two children; (3) He occasionally plays with a large group (three or more children); (4) He usually plays with a larger group (three or more children)". The child's score on each item is recorded on a profile sheet. Description of the scale and rating and scoring instructions are included in a 16-page manual.
NORMS, RELIABILITY, VALIDITY: Manual provides information
SOURCE: Consulting Psychologists Press, Inc., 577 College Avenue, Palo Alto, California 94306
APPROXIMATE COST: $6 for Manual and 25 Test Booklets

Child Behavior Rating Scale (CBRS)

AUTHOR: Russell N. Cassell
DATE: 1962
PURPOSE: To obtain objective behavior ratings in order to assess personality adjustment
AGE RANGE: Kindergarten through third grade

WHO CAN ADMINISTER: Teachers and parents or others who have studied the manual and observed or know directly the behavior of the child (to be interpreted by a clinician)

TIME TO ADMINISTER: Unspecified (rating scale)

DESCRIPTION: The administrator responds to 78 brief statements by rating the child on a scale of 6 values, ranging from Yes to No. The statements are grouped into 5 adjustment areas: self, home, social, school, and physical. Scores obtained in these 5 individual areas are added together to give a Total Adjustment Score. Self, home, and social adjustment scores are based on 20 items each; school adjustment and physical adjustment scores are based on 12 and 6 items respectively. Examples of statements in each of the 5 areas are (A) Self Adjustment: "Often is not very tactful with others."; (B) Home Adjustment: "There is evidence of excessive bad habits in home."; (C) Social Adjustment: "Often plays with children younger than self."; (D) School Adjustment: "Often seems afraid to speak out in class."; (E) Physical Adjustment: "Has uncorrected poor vision or poor hearing."

NORMS, RELIABILITY, VALIDITY: Manual provides detailed information

SOURCE: Western Psychological Services, 12031 Wilshire Boulevard, Los Angeles, California 90025

APPROXIMATE COST: $9 for Manual and 25 Scales

Children's Self-Social Constructs Test: Preschool Form

AUTHORS: Barbara H. Long, Edmund H. Henderson, and Robert C. Ziller

DATE: 1965

PURPOSE: To reflect various aspects of the child's perception of self in relation to others

AGE RANGE: 3 to 7 years

WHO CAN ADMINISTER: Teachers who have studied the manual

TIME TO ADMINISTER: 15 minutes

DESCRIPTION: This test contains 26 items with 1 page of drawings for each item. The drawings depict mother, father, two children (friends), or teacher; in some cases, circles are assigned names of persons. The child responds to questions by putting his/her finger on the preferred drawing. For example, the examiner says "Here is your father and here are your friends. Pretend your finger is you. Put yourself with whichever one you want." On another type of item, the child is told, "These circles are children. Pretend your finger is you. Put yourself wherever you want to." There are 6 kinds of items in all that give scores for esteem; social interest; realism; minority identification; preference for mother, father, teacher, and friend; and identification with mother, father, teacher, and friend. The 44-page manual includes rationale and theoretical background, empirical meanings, and interpretations of findings.

NORMS, RELIABILITY, VALIDITY: Manual provides information
SOURCE: Virginia Research Associates, Ltd., P. O. Box 5501, Charlottesville, Virginia 22902
APPROXIMATE COST: $9 for Manual, Reuseable Pupil Book, 35 Scoring Sheets

Classroom Behavior Inventory — Preschool Form

AUTHORS: E. S. Schaefer and Marianna D. Edgerton
DATE: 1978
PURPOSE: To assess academic competence and social adjustment of children in day care and preschool situations; to provide a method for collecting valid data on the child's classroom behavior from teachers and day care workers
AGE RANGE: 2 to 6 years
WHO CAN ADMINISTER: Teachers who have studied the manual
TIME TO ADMINISTER: 5 to 10 minutes (rating scale)
DESCRIPTION: The preschool form of the CBI is a research version based on 2 inventories developed earlier, 1 for infants and 1 for kindergarten and elementary school children. The inventory consists of 60 brief descriptions of the child's behavior (**Ex:** "Is quickly distracted by noise and activity"). The teacher rates each item on a 5-point scale, ranging from "not at all like" to "very much like." The scoring form indicates which items comprise each of 11 subscales: (1) Verbal Intelligence, (2) Introversion, (3) Considerateness, (4) Dependence, (5) Task Orientation, (6) Apathy, (7) Extroversion, (8) Hostility, (9) Creativity/Curiosity, (10) Distractibility, and (11) Indepen-

dence. There are either 4 or 6 items for each of the subscales except Verbal Intelligence, for which there are 10 items.

NORMS, RELIABILITY, VALIDITY: Information available

SOURCE: Earl S. Schaefer, University of North Carolina, Chapel Hill, North Carolina 27514

APPROXIMATE COST: Available from above source on request

Detroit Adjustment Inventory (DAI) — Delta Form

AUTHOR: Harry J. Baker

DATE: 1954

PURPOSE: To locate or to discover problems or conditions unfavorable to young children and to suggest ways and means of bringing about improvements

AGE RANGE: 5 to 8 years

WHO CAN ADMINISTER: Teachers who have studied the manual and who have had several weeks of classroom experience with the children to be rated

TIME TO ADMINISTER: Unspecified (rating scale)

DESCRIPTION: For each of the 64 items comprising the inventory, the rater selects from 4 descriptions the one that best describes the child. The descriptions range from one that is ideal to one that is very unfavorable. For example, the item about paying attention in school has these choices:

A. Is fair in habits of attention
B. Attention varies, must be reminded
C. Pays good attention most of the time
D. Wanders around, attention very poor

The choices are presented in varying order from item to item in the interest of preventing a response set on the part of the rater.

The first 16 items on the Inventory deal with the child's personal characteristics (speech, cleanliness, truthfulness, etc.). The second, third, and fourth sets of 16 items evaluate the child's reactions to school, community, and home respectively. For the set of items dealing with the child's adjustment to the home environment, the 7-page manual provides a comprehensive list of suggested questions and pointers to use in interviewing parents when complete information about the home has not been secured by other means.

An individual Record Blank and Scoring Key enables the rater to obtain a Status, Social, Emotional, and Ethical score for each of the 4 environments (Self, School, Community, and Home).

A series of 16 remedial leaflets are each keyed to an area covered by 4 specific items on the Inventory. The author suggests that whenever a total score for an area is 10 points or less (the maximum possible score for an area is 16) the pertinent remedial leaflet should be used by the teacher, and also given to the parents, in order to improve the child's adjustment and to improve the relationships between school, home, and community.

NORMS, RELIABILITY, VALIDITY: Information available

SOURCE: Test Division of the Bobbs-Merrill Company, Inc., 4300 West 62nd Street, Indianapolis, Indiana 46268

APPROXIMATE COST: $8 for Package of 35 Inventories

Florida KEY: Elementary Form

AUTHORS: William W. Purkey, Bob N. Cage, and William Graves

DATE: 1973

PURPOSE: To assess the child's perception of his/her "learner" self

AGE RANGE: 2 through 13 years

WHO CAN ADMINISTER: Teachers who have studied the manual

TIME TO Administer: Unspecified (rating scale)

DESCRIPTION: The Elementary Form of the KEY consists of 24 questions about the child's school behavior. The teacher is asked to record whether the child, in comparison with his/her age peers, exhibits the named behavior. A 6-point scale, ranging from Never to Very Often, is used to rate the child. The items cover 4 types of behavior (relating, asserting, investing, and coping) and are stated in positive terms (**Ex:** "Does this student speak up for his/her own ideas?"). Authors indicate that this is a research instrument on which data are still being collected.

NORMS, RELIABILITY, VALIDITY: Information available
SOURCE: Bureau of Educational Research, University of Mississippi, University, Mississippi 38677
APPROXIMATE COST: Available from above source

The Joseph Pre-School and Primary Self Concept Screening Test

AUTHOR: Jack Joseph
DATE: 1979
PURPOSE: To objectively screen and identify children who, due to their negative self-appraisals, may become high risk for learning problems or develop other adjustment difficulties
AGE RANGE: 3-6 to 10-0 years
WHO CAN ADMINISTER: Teachers, paraprofessionals, and others who are thoroughly familiar with administering and scoring the test. The examiner should not be the child's present teacher or one who is personally familiar with the child or members of the family because of the sensitive nature of the material. Trained professionals should be involved in interpreting and reporting test results.
DESCRIPTION: The test administrator begins by showing the child an outline of a boy or girl, depending on the child's sex. Facial features are not included and the child is first requested to draw his/her own face onto the picture. This serves as an Identity Reference Drawing that is displayed for the child as he/she responds to a series of 15 questions. The general procedure is for the examiner to show the child 2 pictures for each question (**Ex:** One picture is of a clean, neat, and well-groomed child while the other picture show a dirty, ragged, and unkempt child). The examiner asks the child to indicate, verbally or by pointing, which one is "most like you." Detailed instructions are given in the manual for administering and scoring. Tables are provided for transferring scores, by age, to classifications ranging from High Positive to High Risk Negative. The face initially drawn on the Identity Reference Drawing may be evaluated for problems in visual-motor coordination and for emotional dysfunctioning. The 66-page manual includes a re-

source guide for self-concept enhancement strategies.

NORMS, RELIABILITY, VALIDITY: Manual provides information

SOURCE: Stoelting Company, 1350 South Kostner Avenue, Chicago, Illinois 60623

APPROXIMATE COST: $27 for Manual, Stimulus Cards, 100 Identity Reference Drawings, and 100 Record Forms

Measurement of Emotional Maturity Scales (MEM)

AUTHOR: Harold Bessell

DATE: 1978

PURPOSE: To measure the child's self-concept, or degree of emotional maturity, in 4 basic component areas

AGE RANGE: 5 to 12 years

WHO CAN ADMINISTER: Teachers who have observed a child for at least 2 months

TIME TO ADMINISTER: Short scale, 8 to 15 minutes; full scale, 20 to 45 minutes

DESCRIPTION: The short form of the MEM contains 70 items and the long form contains 237 items. The items measure the following areas: Awareness (**Ex:** "Copes well with uncertainty"); Relating (**Ex:** "Makes friends easily, and keeps them"); Competence (**Ex:** "Shows self-reliant behavior"); and Integrity (**Ex:** "Willingly carries own share of the work load").

Rating is based on a 5-point scale that ranges from Rarely to Very Often. These ratings are marked on machine scoring sheets and sent to the test publishers, who return a complete profile based on percentile scores. A variety of materials are available, including teacher's manual, prescriptive booklet, sample report profile, parent pamphlets, etc.

NORMS, RELIABILITY, VALIDITY: Information available

SOURCE: Psych/Graphic Publishers, P. O. Box 28027, San Diego, California 92128

APPROXIMATE COST: $6 for 5 reusable Short Form Rating Booklets and Answer Sheets. Cost of machine scoring varies from $1.45 to $1.89 depending on the form and the number of answer sheets to be scored.

Nursery School Behavior Inventory

AUTHOR: Richard N. Walker
DATE: 1962
PURPOSE: To obtain teachers' judgments of behavior of children in their classrooms
AGE RANGE: 2 to 5 years
WHO CAN ADMINISTER: Teachers who have read the instructions
TIME TO ADMINISTER: Unspecified (rating scale)
DESCRIPTION: The Inventory consists of a rating scale of 66 items that describe children's behavior. Names and definitions are given for each item, which the teacher rates on a scale from 1 to 7. The scale provides a description for each level. As an illustration, for the item "Accident Proneness" a score of 1 is given to the child who "Gets far more than his share of bumps, cuts, falls, etc., is repeatedly having some kind of accident." A score of 7 is given to the child who "Never gets hurt."

For the purpose of interpretation, item scores are clustered under the following general descriptions: (1) Energetic, Active; (2) Alert, Curious; (3) Aggressive, Assertive; (4) Fearful, Anxious; (5) Social, Friendly; (6) Excitable, Unstable; (7) Cooperative, Conforming; (8) Cheerful, Expressive; (9) Sensitive, Easily Hurt. Each cluster score is described and discussed, and mean scores by age and sex are given in a table. The Inventory was initially developed to be used in a study on body build and behavior in young children.
NORMS, RELIABILITY, VALIDITY: Information available
SOURCE: May be duplicated from Appendix of *Monograph of the Society for Research in Child Development*, 1962, *Vol. 27, No. 3*. A 5-page discussion of revisions is available from the author: Richard N. Walker, Gesell Institute of Child Development, 310 Prospect Street, New Haven Connecticut 06511
APPROXIMATE COST: See above source

Preschool Behavior Questionnaire

AUTHORS: Lenore Behar and Samuel Stringfield

DATE: 1974

PURPOSE: To identify at an early age children who may be developing behavior problems

AGE RANGE: 3 to 6 years

WHO CAN ADMINISTER: Teachers and other child care workers who have had children in the classroom for at least 6 weeks and who have had special training in child psychology

TIME TO ADMINISTER: Unspecified (checklist)

DESCRIPTION: The Preschool Behavior Questionnaire consists of 30 descriptive statements of child behavior often shown by preschoolers. For example, one item is "Fights with other children." The administrator checks each item according to whether the behavior "does not apply," "applies sometimes," or "certainly applies." Scores are transferred to a profile that shows the total score and also subscores classified according to 3 scales (Hostile-Aggressive, Anxious, and Hyperactive-Distractible). Recommendations for interpretations are given. For example, a child whose total score is above the 90th percentile may be having trouble. Since the items focus on negative characteristics, the authors warn that there is the possibility that results may be misused by teachers to label children if the teachers do not provide for appropriate referrals or treatment. The instrument may also be used as a pre-post measure of children to indicate areas of change or growth during a period of time of at least 3 months.

NORMS, RELIABILITY, VALIDITY: Manual provides information

SOURCE: Learning Institute of North Carolina, 1006 Lamond Avenue, Durham, North Carolina 27701

APPROXIMATE COST: $5 for Manual and 50 Score Sheets

Preschool Self-Concept Picture Test

AUTHOR: Rosestelle B. Woolner

DATE: 1966

PURPOSE: To assess the attitudes that pupils have toward themselves

AGE RANGE: 3 to 7 years

WHO CAN ADMINISTER: Teachers who have studied the manual

TIME TO ADMINISTER: 15 minutes

DESCRIPTION: This self-concept test consists of a set of 10 pairs of pictures, each pair depicting a child with a "positive" and "negative" characteristic. There are 4 sets of plates depicting black and white children of both sexes. The characteristics shown are: Dirty vs. Clean, Active vs. Passive, Aggressive vs. Nonaggressive, Afraid vs. Unafraid, Strong vs. Weak, Acceptance vs. Rejection Of, Unhappy vs. Happy, Group Rejection vs. Group Acceptance, Sharing vs. Not Sharing, Dependence vs. Independence. On 3 of the pairs, sex differences in characteristics are noted; i.e., scoring for *positive* characteristics of girls are Passive, Non-Aggressive, and Weak.

When administering the test, the examiner asks the child, "Which boy (girl) are you?" After the child points to one of the 2 pictures, the examiner asks, "Which boy (girl) would you like to be?" Scoring on the answer sheet shows both the consciously attributed characteristics and the consciously "wished for" characteristics. Agreements and disagreements between the self-concept and the ideal self-concept are also to be noted. Results can be compared with tables in the manual. The manual also includes a discussion of how the teacher might observe whether a child's behavior is consistent with responses, whether he/she seems to want to change, and how the teacher might facilitate positive change.

NORMS, RELIABILITY, VALIDITY: Manual provides information
SOURCE: Rosestelle B. Woolner, 3551 Aurora Circle, Memphis, Tennessee 38111
APPROXIMATE COST: $20 for Picture Books, Manual, and 25 Record Forms

Primary Self-Concept Inventory (PSCI)

AUTHORS: Douglas G. Muller and Robert Leonetti
DATE: 1975
PURPOSE: To evaluate several aspects of self-concept relevant to school success
AGE RANGE: Kindergarten through sixth grade (also 4-year-olds who have had preschool training)
WHO CAN ADMINISTER: Teachers who have studied the test manual

TIME TO ADMINISTER: Unspecified
DESCRIPTION: This Inventory may be administered individually or to small groups. There are 18 nonverbal items with pictures for each item. The teacher reads a statement and the child draws a circle around the picture that is "most like" the child. Usually there are two contrasting pictures, one showing one or more children in a positive role and the other illustrating a negative role. For example, one picture shows a child at school playing with other children and the other shows the child playing alone. There are separate booklets for boys and for girls. There are 3 domain scores: Personal-Self, Social-Self, and Intellectual-Self. Both the total score and the domain scores may be translated to percentiles. The authors emphasize that most children obtain relatively high scores and that usually only those with low scores need further follow-up. The test manual includes questions in Spanish as well as English.
NORMS, RELIABILITY, VALIDITY: Manual provides information
SOURCE: Teaching Resources Corporation, 50 Pond Park Road, Hingham, Massachusetts, 02043
APPROXIMATE COST: $20 for Manual, Technical Report, and 20 Test Forms

Psychiatric Behavior Scale

AUTHORS: William F. Barker, Louise Sandler, Agnes Bornemann, Gail Knight, Frederick Humphrey, and Steven Risen
DATE: Undated
PURPOSE: To assess longitudinally the emotional development of preschool children with problems
AGE RANGE: 2-6 to 6-6 years
WHO CAN ADMINISTER: Day care workers who have read the instructions and who have had at least one month of continuous contact with the child
TIME TO ADMINISTER: Unspecified (checklist)
DESCRIPTION: There are 5 bipolar items, 1 unipolar item, and 8 yes-no questions comprising the scale. Each of the 6 major items consists of 5 to 8 descriptive statements (the rater chooses the one that best describes the child). Areas assessed by the 6 items are: Expression of Aggression, Interpersonal Relation-

ships, Dependence, Impulse Control, Reaction to Stress, and Need for Communication. Depending on the rating given on the bipolar items, the child's behavior in any one area may be described as either typical or tending toward one or the other extreme. For example, on the Impulse Control item, rating may range from No Control at one extreme to Too Controlled at the other extreme. The unipolar item, Need for Communication, elicits information regarding the way in which the child communicates his/her needs. The yes-no questions concern such problems as head-banging, poor coordination, and elimination accidents.

Instructions are attached to the 2-page test form. Users of the scale are asked to return the completed checklists to the first author (see Source) for scoring and a printout of subscores and averages.

NORMS, RELIABILITY, VALIDITY: Information available

SOURCE: William Barker, Center for Preschool Services, Room 469, Franklin Institute Research Laboratories, 20th and the Parkway, Philadelphia, Pennsylvania 19103

APPROXIMATE COST: Available from the above source

Pupil Behavior Inventory (PBI): Early Education Version

AUTHORS: Rosemary Carri and Norma Radin

DATE: 1973

PURPOSE: To identify problems visible to teachers and others which may be useful diagnostically for school personnel who provide special services to students

AGE RANGE: 3 to 5 years

WHO CAN ADMINISTER: Teachers who have studied the manual or attended a workshop (interpretation should be by clinicians or teachers with training)

TIME TO ADMINISTER: 15 minutes

DESCRIPTION: The Inventory consists of 44 items that measure 8 areas of social behavior: Classroom Misconduct, Creative Inquisitiveness, Good Student Behavior, Teacher Dependence, Poor Physical Condition, Academic Motivation, Antisocial, and Problematic Socioemotional State. Ratings for each item (**Ex:** "Influences others toward troublemaking") are made on a

5-point scale ranging from Very Frequently to Very Infrequently. Scoring is accomplished by using a scoring mask for each area. Results can be used by teachers to evaluate the particular needs of the child. Results may also measure changes before and after intervention programs.

NORMS, RELIABILITY, VALIDITY: Information available
SOURCE: Professor Norma Radin, School of Social Work, University of Michigan, Ann Arbor, Michigan 48109
APPROXIMATE COST: Available from above source

School Behavior Checklist

AUTHOR: Lovick C. Miller
DATE: 1977
PURPOSE: To evaluate the child's behavior in school
AGE RANGE: 4 to 6 years (Form A)
WHO CAN ADMINISTER: Teachers who have read the instructions (to be interpreted by clinicians, school psychologists, or other testing specialists)
TIME TO ADMINISTER: 10 minutes
DESCRIPTION: The main section of this 4-page checklist consists of 104 true-false items (Ex: "Teases other children"). Items are interpreted in terms of Need Achievement, Aggression, Anxiety, Cognitive or Academic Deficit, Hostile Isolation, Extraversion, Normal Irritability, School Distractibility, and Total Disability. The test form also includes general information questions and 11 items requiring global judgments by the teacher, such as "How would you rate this pupil's social and emotional adjustment?" The Checklist is to be used to provide clinicians with an assessment of the child's behavioral repertoire in school.
NORMS, RELIABILITY, VALIDITY: Information available
SOURCE: Western Psychological Services, 12031 Wilshire Boulevard, Los Angeles, California 90025
APPROXIMATE COST: $30 for Manual, Scoring Templates, 25 Reusable Questionnaires, and 100 Answer Sheets

Category 7

SPEECH/HEARING/VISION

Denver Articulation Screening Exam (DASE)

AUTHOR: Amelia F. Drumwright and William K. Frankenburg
DATE: 1971
PURPOSE: To discriminate between significant development delay and normal variations in the acquisition of speech sounds; to detect common abnormal conditions
AGE RANGE: 2-6 to 6 years
WHO CAN ADMINISTER: Speech pathologists and others who have reached the degree of proficiency designated in the DASE Training Package
TIME TO ADMINISTER: 5 minutes
DESCRIPTION: The DASE consists of a 1-page form containing a list of 22 words with an underlined sound or blend under each word. The test assesses the child's ability to pronounce 30 sound elements. The examiner pronounces the word and asks the child to repeat it. (Simple line illustrations are provided on cards to be used with children who are shy or hard to test.) The back of the test form shows the child's percentile and cut-off point, based on age, between normal and abnormal. The examiner also evaluates the child's general verbal intelligibility on a 4-point scale, which is scored as Normal or Abnormal based on age. The reference manual includes a table showing percent of sample children passing each sound, based on age and cultural group (Anglo, Black, and Mexican-American). Instructional materials, including films, are available for training examiners in order that the test will be used properly. The test was developed at the University of Colorado Medical Center.
NORMS, RELIABILITY, VALIDITY: Manual provides information
SOURCE: The LADOCA Project and Publishing Foundation,

Inc., East 51st Avenue and Lincoln Street, Denver, Colorado 80216
Approximate Cost: $5 for Picture Cards, Reference Manual, and 25 Test Forms

Denver Audiometric Screening Test (DAST)

Authors: Amelia F. Drumwright and William K. Frankenburg
Date: 1973
Purpose: To identify children who are likely to have a serious hearing loss
Age Range: 3 to 6 years
Who can Administer: Clinicians, specialists, teachers, paraprofessionals, and volunteers who have reached degree of proficiency designated in the DAST training package
Time to Administer: 5 to 10 minutes
Description: The DAST involves testing for reaction to 3 sound frequencies on a pure-tone audiometer. Each ear is tested and results are shown on the 1-page form as Passing, Failing, or Uncertain. Specific suggestions are given for testing young children (use of toys, blocks, etc., instead of asking the child to raise his/her hand). The reference manual explains the technique of audiometric screening and gives instruction for scoring and interpreting results, i.e. whether the child should be referred for further testing. Instructional materials, including a film, are available for training examiners in order that the test will be used properly. The test was developed at the University of Colorado Medical Center.
Norms, Reliability, Validity: Information available
Source: The LADOCA Project and Publishing Foundation, Inc., East 51st Avenue and Lincoln Street, Denver, Colorado 80216
Approximate Cost: $3 for Reference Manual and 25 Test Forms

Denver Eye Screening Test (DEST)

Authors: John Barker, Arnold Goldstein, and William K. Frankenburg

DATE: 1972

PURPOSE: To detect problems in visual acuity and non-straight eyes (strabismus, refractive error, and amblyopia)

AGE RANGE: 6 months to 6 years

WHO CAN ADMINISTER: Clinicians, specialists, teachers, and paraprofessionals who have reached proficiency designated in the DEST Training Package

TIME TO ADMINISTER: 5 to 10 minutes

DESCRIPTION: The DEST uses a series of established measures of visual assessment. There are 3 tests of visual acuity (the E Test, Picture Card Test, and Fixation Test), each for a specific age range; and 3 procedures for non-straight eyes (questioning the mother about the appearance of the child's eyes, the Cover Test, and the Pupillary Light Reflex Test). The test kit includes a set of picture cards, the illiterate E card, plastic occluder, spinning toy, and a measuring cord. Scoring is in terms of Normal, Abnormal, and Untestable. Results are used to determine if the child needs no further screening, should be rescreened within a few weeks, or needs a complete eye examination by an eye specialist. The reference manual explains administration and interpretation. Instructional materials, including films, are available for training administrators in order that the test will be used properly. The DEST was developed at the University of Colorado Medical Center.

NORMS, RELIABILITY, VALIDITY: Information available

SOURCE: The LADOCA Project and Publishing Foundation, Inc., East 51st Avenue and Lincoln Street, Denver, Colorado 80216

APPROXIMATE COST: $9 for Test Kit, Reference Manual, and 25 Test Forms

Home Eye Test for Preschoolers

AUTHORS: National Society for the Prevention of Blindness, Inc.

DATE: 1975

PURPOSE: To screen for possible visual problems

AGE RANGE: 3 to 6 years

WHO CAN ADMINISTER: Parents and teachers who have read the instructions

TIME TO ADMINISTER: Unspecified

DESCRIPTION: The test consists of a Snellen Illiterate "E" Chart with step-by-step instructions for administering. A brief statement about the need for early vision screening is followed by suggestions for assembling materials (a cup to cover the child's eye, tack to hang chart, scissors, and pencil), preparing the setting, teaching the child appropriate responses (pointing in 4 different directions), testing the vision, interpreting results, and making referrals. Authors stress that this test in no way takes the place of a professional eye examination, which they recommend for every child before entering school.

NORMS, RELAIBILITY, VALIDITY: None reported with the test

SOURCE: National Society for the Prevention of Blindness, 79 Madison Avenue, New York, New York 10016

APPROXIMATE COST: Available from above source on request

Riley Articulation and Language Test: Revised

AUTHOR: Glyndon D. Riley

DATE: 1971

PURPOSE: To rapidly screen children in order to identify those with speech problems

AGE RANGE: Kindergarten to second grade

WHO CAN ADMINISTER: Speech pathologists, teachers, and others who have sufficient knowledge of articulation disorders to recognize speech deviations quickly

TIME TO ADMINISTER: 3 minutes

DESCRIPTION: The test is divided into four sections:

1. *Language Proficiency.* The examiner asks the child to tell a familiar story and while the child is talking the examiner completes a 4-item checklist (**Ex:** "Willingness to talk").

2. *Language Intelligibility.* As the child tells the story, the examiner also checks a 5-point scale according to his/her estimate of percent of intelligibility of the child's speech relative to age and culture.

3. *Articulation Function.* The child repeats 8 words, one at a time, after the examiner. Scoring for the underlined sound in each word is according to substitution, omission, distor-

tion, and whether or not correct responses were produced on extra tries.

4. *Language Function.* The child is given 2 chances to repeat each of 6 sentences. Testing is stopped after 2 consecutive failures.

There is also a 6-item checklist for the examiner's Yes-No answers regarding several types of additional problems, such as stuttering. Instructions are provided in the 4-page test form and in the 5-page manual for interpreting scores on each of the 4 sections.

NORMS, RELIABILITY, VALIDITY: Manual provides information
SOURCE: Western Psychological Services, 12031 Wilshire Boulevard, Los Angeles, California 90025
APPROXIMATE COST: $9 for Manual and 25 Test Forms

Test of Auditory Analysis Skills (TAAS)

AUTHOR: Jerome Rosner
DATE: 1975
PURPOSE: To test a child's auditory-perceptual skills and to identify goals for teaching these skills
AGE RANGE: Kindergarten through third grade
WHO CAN ADMINISTER: Teachers who have studied the instructions
TIME TO ADMINISTER: Unspecified
DESCRIPTION: In the TAAS the examiner pronounces a word that the child repeats; the examiner then asks the child to omit a certain part of the word (**Ex:** Child repeats "cowboy," then is asked to "Say it again and don't say 'boy'"). There are 13 words in the test; most of them involve asking the child to omit a sound, such as to omit /m/ in "meat." Testing is stopped after 2 consecutive failures. A table on the 1-page record form indicates the child's estimated grade level based on number of correct responses. For example, if there are 1, 2, or 3 correct responses the child is classified at the kindergarten level. If the child falls below the expected level of performance, it is suggested that he/she be taught to improve performance. Material is available for training in discrimination.
NORMS, RELIABILITY, VALIDITY: Information available

Source: Academic Therapy Publication, 20 Commercial Boulevard, Novato, California 94947

Approximate Cost: $2 for 25 Test/Record Forms, which include instructions to the examiner

Tree/Bee Test of Auditory Discrimination

Author: Janet B. Fudala

Date: 1978

Purpose: To provide a wide range of tasks for persons who may be suspected of having an auditory discrimination problem

Age Range: 3 years to adult

Who can Administer: Teachers who have studied the manual and practiced by giving the test to at least 5 persons

Time to Administer: 10 to 15 minutes

Description: This test may be given individually or in small groups. For individual administration, a flip book of pictures is used, and the child points to the appropriate response. There is a pretest vocabulary check of 18 words; the child is taught any pictures that he identifies incorrectly. The test consists of the following types of materials:

1. Words (**Ex:** Examiner shows pictures of a cane, a can, and a cone and asks child to point to the cane.)
2. Phrases (**Ex:** Examiner shows pictures of a monkey on a bed and a monkey on a sled and asks child to point to the monkey on a sled.)
3. Pairs (**Ex:** Examiner asks child to select picture of beet/beet from pictures of boot/boot, boot/beet, and beet/boot.)
4. Comprehension (**Ex:** Examiner tells a brief story and asks child to point to all the pictures he/she heard in the story.)
5. Pointing to Words (**Ex:** Examiner asks child to point to one picture, such as "cake," in a group of pictures.)
6. Same-Different (**Ex:** Examiner pronounces "four/pour" and asks child to indicate if the words are the same or different.)
7. Letters (**Ex:** Examiner asks child to repeat "P-X-N.")

Scoring is classified on the test form according to several criteria, such as whether the child discriminated vowels and consonants. The test form includes a table for translating total raw score to age and grade equivalents and also includes space for showing the percent of correct discriminations of sounds, words, phrases, etc. Recommendations are made in the 47-page manual for interpretation and follow-up. The manual also includes annotated bibliographies of auditory tests and remedial materials.

NORMS, RELIABILITY, VALIDITY: Manual provides information

SOURCE: Academic Therapy Publications, 28 Commercial Boulevard, Novato, California 94947

APPROXIMATE COST: $30 for Flip-Book, Manual, and 10 each of Recording Forms 1 and 2 for individual administration

Category 8

VISUAL MOTOR/VISUAL PERCEPTUAL

Developmental Test of Visual-Motor Integration (VMI)

AUTHORS: Keith E. Beery and Norman A. Buktenica
DATE: 1967
PURPOSE: To measure the degree to which visual perception and motor behavior are integrated in young children
AGE RANGE: 2 to 15 years
WHO CAN ADMINISTER: Teachers who study the manual
TIME TO ADMINISTER: 15 to 20 minutes
DESCRIPTION: There are 2 forms of this test, one for younger children and one for older children. The test booklet for ages 2 to 8 years includes 15 geometric designs of increasing difficulty, beginning with a straight vertical line. The child copies the design in a space directly below the printed one. However, the test may also be administered by using a set of cards instead of a test booklet. Criteria for passing or failing are described and illustrated in the manual, and testing is usually discontinued after the child has failed 3 consecutive designs. Age equivalents for raw scores are given by sex, and additional developmental data from other sources are given for children under 3 years of age. The 75-page manual includes a discussion of individualized remediation of visual-motor difficulties. Resources for remediation are listed and worksheets are available.
NORMS, RELIABILITY, VALIDITY: Information available in manual and accompanying monograph
SOURCE: Follett Publishing Company, 1010 West Washington Boulevard, Chicago, Illinois 60607
APPROXIMATE COST: $21 for Manual, 15 Short Form Tests, Monograph, and Stimulus Cards

Frostig Developmental Test of Visual Perception (DTVP)

AUTHORS: Marianne Frostig and Associates
DATE: 1966

PURPOSE: To identify children who need special perceptual training

AGE RANGE: 3 to 8 years

WHO CAN ADMINISTER: Teachers and psychometricians who have studied the manual; clinicians (for additional diagnosis)

TIME TO ADMINISTER: Unspecified

DESCRIPTION: This paper-and-pencil test consists of 5 subtests of visual perception:

1. Eye-Motor Coordination (**Ex:** Child draws straight and curved lines between increasingly narrow boundaries)
2. Figure-Ground (**Ex:** Child traces around intersecting and hidden geometric forms in increasingly complex grounds)
3. Form Constancy (**Ex:** Child traces around geometric forms presented in a variety of sizes, textures, and positions in space)
4. Position in Space (**Ex:** Child differentiates between figures in an identical position and those in a reverse or rotated position)
5. Spatial Relations (**Ex:** Child copies patterns by linking dots)

Specific scoring instructions are given in the manual. Scores are translated to a Perceptual Quotient and suggestions are given for determining the need for further testing. The test may be given individually or to small groups. A program to develop and expand children's perceptual skills is available.

NORMS, RELIABILITY, VALIDITY: Information available

SOURCE: Consulting Psychologists Press, Inc., 577 College Avenue, Palo Alto, California 94306

APPROXIMATE COST: $10 for Examiner's Kit, which contains Manual, Monograph, Plastic Score Keys, Set of Demonstration Cards, 10 Test Booklets

Jordan Left-Right Reversal Test

AUTHOR: Brian T. Jordan

DATE: 1974

PURPOSE: To measure letter and number reversals in the area of visual receptive functioning

AGE RANGE: 5-0 to 12-11 years

Who can Administer: Teachers and clinicians who have studied the manual

Time to Administer: 25 minutes

Description: This test includes 2 levels. The first level, for children 5 through 8 years, consists of testing for recognition of reversals of letters and of numbers. The section concerning letters shows 3 rows of printed letters, some of which are reversed. For the pre-first-grade child, the examiner prints the first letter correctly on a separate sheet and asks the child to mark through the first letter on the test form if it is "backward." This method is followed for each letter. The same procedure is followed for the section on recognition of reversal of numbers. Scores are converted to percentiles according to age and sex and a Developmental Age can be estimated. The 48-page manual discusses interpretation and gives recommendations for children who have high error scores.

Norms, Reliability, Validity: Manual provides information

Source: Academic Therapy Publications, 20 Commercial Boulevard, Novato, California 94947

Approximate Cost: $7 for Manual and 25 Score Sheets

The Moore Eye-Hand Coordination Test: Preschool Form

Author: Joseph E. Moore

Date: 1952

Purpose: To measure the speed and accuracy with which an individual can coordinate small muscle movements involving eye-hand activity

Age Range: 2 to 6-6 years

Who can Administer: Teachers who have studied the test manual

Time to Administer: Unspecified

Description: This test involves use of testing equipment that consists of a box with 4 compartments; 2 hold 8 marbles each and 2 have 8 holes each into which the marbles are to be placed. Testing is conducted as a game, in which the child is encouraged to work as fast as possible to place the marbles in a specified manner in the holes. The score is the total time in seconds it takes the child to complete 3 trials of the test. The total score translates to percentile ranks by age. A manual of directions for the Preschool Form supplements the regular manual for older children and adults.

NORMS, RELIABILITY, VALIDITY: Manual provides information
SOURCE: Joseph E. Moore & Associates, Perry Drive, R. F. D. 12, Box 309, Gainesville, Georgia 30501
APPROXIMATE COST: $30 for Manuals and test equipment

Motor-Free Visual Perception Test (MVPT)

AUTHORS: Ronald P. Colarusso and Donald D. Hammill
DATE: 1972
PURPOSE: To measure visual perception without motor involvement
AGE RANGE: 4 to 8 years
WHO CAN ADMINISTER: Teachers, psychologists, and educational specialists who have studied the manual
TIME TO ADMINISTER: 10 minutes
DESCRIPTION: The MVPT consists of 36 items based on 5 components of visual perception: spatial relationships, visual discrimination, figure-ground, visual closure, and visual memory. Most of the items involve a line drawing followed by 4 drawings from which the child chooses the correct response by pointing. Examples of items are: locating the exact stimulus figure among the 4 alternatives; locating the stimulus figure among 4 alternatives in which the figures are smaller, bigger, darker, or rotated; examining a figure for 5 seconds and then finding it on a second page among 4 alternatives; identifying the alternative that looks like the stimulus figure if it were to be completed; and identifying a figure that is different from the other figures. The drawings are in a large 50-page spiral-bound book. Total number of correct responses can be translated to a perceptual age and to a perceptual quotient by reference to tables in the manual. The 32-page manual includes discussion of development of the test items, educational implications and uses, and references for remedial techniques.

NORMS, RELIABILITY, VALIDITY: Manual provides information
SOURCE: Academic Therapy Publications, 20 Commercial Boulevard, Novato, California 94947

APPROXIMATE COST: $18 for Booklet with Test Plates, Manual, and 25 Scoring Sheets

Pre-Reading Screening Procedures: Revised Edition

AUTHOR: Beth H. Slingerland
DATE: 1977
PURPOSE: To find, among children having average to superior intelligence, the ones who show auditory, visual, and/or kinesthetic difficulties that often indicate specific language disability
AGE RANGE: Kindergarten or first grade children who have not yet been introduced to reading
WHO CAN ADMINISTER: Teachers who have studied the manual
TIME TO ADMINISTER: Unspecified (three sessions recommended)
DESCRIPTION: The Screening Procedures are described as a group test, which may be given individually. The test consists of 12 subtests divided into visual and auditory approaches, some of which involve motor activity. Examples of visual procedures are: writing name; drawing picture of self; copying designs, letters, and numbers; and drawing several types of figures from memory. Examples of auditory and auditory-visual procedures are: indicating whether words pronouned by the examiner sound the same or different, marking a picture whose name begins with the sound pronounced by the examiner, and copying a pronounced letter to indicate the sound was understood.

Scores on each subtest are translated into five ratings ranging from Low to High. These ratings and other information are shown on a summary sheet. A teacher observation sheet is also completed; it includes several items under such headings as Attention Span, Language, and Coordination. This sheet is based on the teacher's general knowledge of the child and is used in conjunction with the summary sheet to make evaluations of each child. The 90-page manual includes discussion of the evaluation procedures, which are based on the Orton-Gillingham rationale of recognizing and teaching children with specific learning disabilities. Final conclusions are classified according to degree of readiness for beginning first grade or need for further observation, testing, or referral. Teaching materials are available.

NORMS, RELIABILITY, VALIDITY: None reported in manual
SOURCE: Educators Publishing Service, Inc., 75 Moulton Street, Cambridge, Massachusetts 02138
APPROXIMATE COST: $15 for manual, 12 Test Booklets and Forms, Cards and Wall Charts

Shape-O Ball Test

AUTHORS: Jerry R. Thomas and Brad S. Chissom
DATE: 1972
PURPOSE: To measure certain perceptual-motor abilities (shape-recognition, perceptual match, and hand-eye coordination), which closely relate to academic readiness
AGE RANGE: 4 to 9 years
WHO CAN ADMINISTER: Teachers who have studied the instruction sheet and paraprofessionals who have been trained to administer the instrument
TIME TO ADMINISTER: 5 minutes
DESCRIPTION: The test involves the use of a plastic hollow sphere with different geometrically shaped holes in the surface. Plastic geometric pieces are scattered randomly, and the child's task is to place the pieces in the holes as fast as possible. The child is timed as he/she inserts the pieces. Score is total time based on 4 trials. An information sheet on research findings is provided with the instruction sheet.
NORMS, RELIABILITY, VALIDITY: Information available
SOURCE: Jerry R. Thomas or Brad S. Chissom, Georgia Southern College, Statesboro, Georgia 30458
APPROXIMATE COST: Administration, scoring, and research material available from the above source. $5 for Shape-O Ball, Tupperware, A Division of Dart Industries, Inc., Orlando, Florida 32802

Simkov Perceptual Organization Inventory

AUTHOR: J. P. Kovacevich
DATE: 1973

PURPOSE: To classify children on the basis of their perceptual maturity and to indicate their readiness for work involving perceptual-motor skills

AGE RANGE: 5 to 9 years

WHO CAN ADMINISTER: Teachers who have studied the manual and paraprofessionals who have been trained to administer this instrument

TIME TO ADMINISTER: Unspecified

DESCRIPTION: The 4-page booklet contains 15 designs that the child copies in an adjoining space. Examples of material to be copied are: geometric forms, designs formed by connecting dots, numerals, letters, and words. The designs are of increasing difficulty, with each keyed to an estimated age. The age level assigned to the last correct drawing is considered to be the child's Perceptual Motor Age. Directions are given for interpretations. It is suggested that the Inventory be given during the first 2 weeks of kindergarten for identifying problems and grouping children. It can then be given at the end of kindergarten to measure growth in perceptual organization. The manual includes a section on children's growth and development and a section that describes a perceptual training program.

NORMS, RELIABILITY, VALIDITY: None reported in manual

SOURCE: Antof Educational Supplies, P. O. Box 5161, Akron, Ohio

APPROXIMATE COST: $8 for Manual and 25 Test Forms

Test of Visual Analysis Skills (TVAS)

AUTHOR: Jerome Rosner

DATE: 1975

PURPOSE: To assess a child's visual perceptual skills in such a way that the test items can be used as teaching objectives

AGE RANGE: Preschool through second grade

WHO CAN ADMINISTER: Teachers who have studied the instruction sheet

TIME TO ADMINISTER: Unspecified

DESCRIPTION: The TVAS consists of 18 patterns that the child is to copy. The initial patterns are formed by lines that connect dots, and the child copies each pattern on a separate set of dots. The test is stopped when the child makes errors on two successive designs. Scoring is based on number of correct patterns copied; a table on the front of the 11-page test booklet indicates at what grade level this places the child. For example, a score of 1 or 2 places the child at the preschool level and scores of 3 through 7 place the child at the kindergarten level. If the child's skills are inadequate, it is suggested that the child be taught to improve performance through proper visual-motor training. A text, which may be ordered separately, describes remedial procedures.

NORMS, RELIABILITY, VALIDITY: Information available in Technical Report

SOURCE: Academic Therapy Publications, 20 Commercial Boulevard, Novato, California 94947

APPROXIMATE COST: $5 for 10 Test Booklets, which include instructions to the examiner

The 3-D Test for Visualization Skill

AUTHOR: Grace Petitclerc
DATE: 1972
PURPOSE: To measure the child's ability to visualize
AGE RANGE: 3 to 8 years
WHO CAN ADMINISTER: Classroom teachers who have studied the test manual
TIME TO ADMINISTER: 20 minutes
DESCRIPTION: This test, based on Piagetian principles, involves the use of a set of colored three-dimensional geometric shapes (sphere, pyramid, and cube) in 2 sizes. There are 3 levels of testing: the first level involves shape identification, size perception, and visual equilibrium; the second level involves visual memory and operational imagery; and the third level involves image transformation. Preschool children are not expected to do well past the first part of Level II. The first test of Level I requires the child to draw and to answer questions about objects that he/she has been allowed to manipulate without seeing. In the second and third tests the child is asked to look at, handle, and draw the three-dimensional shapes and is then

questioned regarding relative size and position of the objects. Level II tests the child's ability (1) to relate the geometric forms to each other by making an arrangement with them and then to draw that arrangement from memory, and (2) to creatively play with the objects. Specific instructions are given for scoring verbal responses and for scoring drawings. The 86-page manual includes a discussion of expectations for development of mental imagery and a table that makes it possible to compare an individual child's scores with median scores based on age. The manual also includes suggestions to the teacher for developing the child's skill of visualization.

NORMS, RELIABILITY, VALIDITY: Manual provides information
SOURCE: Academic Therapy Publications, 20 Commerical Boulevard, Novato, California 94947
APPROXIMATE COST: $27 for set of solid forms, Manual, 25 Student Checklists, and 25 Individual Scoring Sheets

Visual Efficiency Scale

AUTHOR: N. C. Barrago
DATE: 1970
PURPOSE: To determine the level of efficiency at which visual stimuli can be discriminated and perceived accurately
AGE RANGE: Preschool and older
WHO CAN ADMINISTER: Teachers who have studied the manual
TIME TO ADMINISTER: Unspecified
DESCRIPTION: The Scale contains 48 items involving visual tasks. Each item consists of a stimulus design, which is followed by 4 or 5 designs from which the child chooses according to the examiner's instructions, such as "like" or "not like" the initial design. There are 4 sections, which cover 17 objectives:

1. Section I. Discrimination of geometric form, object contour, light-dark intensity, size, and position
2. Section II. Discrimination of size, object, and abstract figure detail
3. Section III. Visual closure, spatial perspective, discrimination of object, and abstract figure details
4. Section IV. Discrimination of size, position, sequence,

and relationships of letter and word symbols and groups of symbols

A profile sheet is provided to plot performances on each section in order to get a picture of the child's visual efficiency level, which is categorized as Satisfactory, Marginal, or Low. The profile may be used to note strengths and weaknesses and to plan a prescriptive teaching schedule for each child. A comprehensive teacher's guide describes activities and materials for each of the 17 objectives. Individual initial assessment is recommended but 2 or 3 children may be handled as a group in reassessment periods.

NORMS, RELIABILITY, VALIDITY: Information available
SOURCE: American Printing House for the Blind, Inc., P. O. Box 6085, Louisville, Kentucky 40206
APPROXIMATE COST: $9 for Teacher's Guide, 10 copies of the Scale, and Examiner's Directions

Visual Memory Scale

AUTHORS: James L. Carroll
DATE: 1975
PURPOSE: To measure short-term visual memory
AGE RANGE: 5 through 6 years
WHO CAN ADMINISTER: Teachers who have studied the manual, psychologists, and learning disability specialists
TIME TO ADMINISTER: Unspecified
DESCRIPTION: The scale consists of 25 items. The examiner first shows the child a design printed on a 6 by 4 inch card; after waiting 5 seconds, the examiner shows the child another card and asks him/her to indicate which of 4 designs is the one previously shown. The designs consist of various types of geometric shapes. Total score, based on errors, may be compared with norms according to age.

NORMS, RELIABILITY, VALIDITY: Information available
SOURCE: Carroll Publications, 201 East Grand Avenue, Mt. Pleasant, Michigan 48858
APPROXIMATE COST: $10 for Manual, 25 Scoring Blanks, and Test Cards

Part Two

Group Administered Instruments

FORMAT USED FOR DESCRIPTIONS

Group administered instruments are generally used with children in kindergarten or early first-grade settings. This section contains brief descriptions of 41 such instruments. An explanation of the format used for these descriptions follows.

TITLE: Complete name of test, followed by acronyms (if used) and subtitle

AUTHOR: Names of major authors or developers

DATE: Date of publication

SOURCE: Name and address of publisher

AGE/GRADE: Ages or grades for which the instrument was designed

DESCRIPTION: Includes the major purpose of the test, names of subtests or areas assessed, and some indication of time required to administer.

Category 1

COGNITIVE

American School Intelligence Test: Primary Form

AUTHORS: Willis E. Pratt, H. R. Trabue, Rutherford B. Porter, and George A. W. Stouffer, Jr.
DATE: 1964
SOURCE: Bobbs-Merrill Educational Publishing, 4300 West 62nd Street, Indianapolis, Indiana 46206
AGE/GRADE: Kindergarten through third grade
DESCRIPTION: This test is part of an intelligence testing program (K-12). The 7 subtests are Analogies, Arithmetic Problems, Sentence Vocabulary, Nonverbal Analogies, Sentence Ingenuity, Arithmetic Ingenuity, and Synonyms and Antonyms. There are two forms available and the test is untimed.

California Short-Form Test of Mental Maturity: Level O (CTMM-SF)

AUTHORS: Elizabeth T. Sullivan, Willis W. Clark, and Ernest W. Tiegs
DATE: 1963
SOURCE: CTB/McGraw-Hill, Del Monte Research Park, Monterey, California 93940
AGE/GRADE: Kindergarten and entering first grade
DESCRIPTION: This group test of mental ability is part of a series of tests for use with kindergarten through adult age groups. In Level O, the teacher reads a short story (about 3 minutes long) to the children and then asks them questions about the story. Questions cover such areas as opposites, similarities, anaogies, numerical values, number problems, verbal comprehension, and delayed recall. Children mark their answers in an 11-page test booklet that can be completed in 45 minutes.

Cognitive Abilities Test: Primary I

AUTHORS: Robert L. Thorndike, Elizabeth P. Hagen, and Irving Lorge
DATE: 1971
SOURCE: Houghton-Mifflin, 666 Miami Circle, N. E., Atlanta, Georgia 30324
AGE/GRADE: Kindergarten through first grade
DESCRIPTION: This instrument is part of a series (K-12) of tests designed to measure a child's scholastic aptitude and abstract reasoning ability. Primary I uses pictorial materials and oral instructions and contains 4 subtests: Oral Vocabulary, Relational Concepts, Multi-Mental Concepts, and Quantitative Concepts. The regular form requires 12 to 16 minutes each for 4 separate sessions. A short form is also available.

Culture Fair Series: Scale I

AUTHORS: Raymond B. Cattell and A. K. S. Cattell
DATE: 1967
SOURCE: Institute for Personality and Ability Testing, Inc., 1602 Coronado Drive, Champaign, Illinois 61820
AGE/GRADE: 4 to 8 years
DESCRIPTION: This instrument is part of a series of tests, for ages 4 years through adulthood, designed to measure intelligence. Scale I consists of 8 subtests. Four of the subtests are administered individually and 4 are administered in groups. The tests were designed to eliminate cultural bias as much as possible and consist of mostly nonverbal responses that indicate a child's ability to perceive relationships in shapes and figures. Testing time is 22 minutes.

Henmon-Nelson Tests of Mental Ability: Primary Battery

AUTHORS: Martin J. Nelson and Joseph L. French
DATE: 1973
SOURCE: Houghton Mifflin, 666 Miami Circle, N. E., Atlanta, Georgia 30324
AGE/GRADE: Kindergarten through second grade

DESCRIPTION: This instrument is part of a series of tests (K-12). The purpose of the Primary Battery is to measure verbal and quantitative skills important in assessing readiness for school work. The battery consists of 3 short subtests: Listening, Picture Vocabulary, Size and Number. Twenty-five to 30 minutes are required for testing.

Kuhlmann-Anderson Tests: Kindergarten Level

AUTHORS: F. Kuhlmann and Rose G. Anderson
DATE: 1967
SOURCE: Scholastic Testing Service, Inc., 480 Meyer Road, Bensenville, Illinois 60106
AGE/GRADE: Kindergarten
DESCRIPTION: This instrument is part of a series of tests (K-12) designed to assess school learning aptitude. The kindergarten level is made up of cognitive tasks that are measures of school learning ability. Testing is completed in 50 to 75 minutes.

Metropolitan Achievement Tests: Preprimer and Primer

AUTHORS: Irving H. Balow, Roger Farr, Thomas P. Hogan, and George A. Prescott
DATE: 1978
SOURCE: Psychological Corporation, 757 Third Avenue, New York, New York 10017
AGE/GRADE: Kindergarten through first grade
DESCRIPTION: These instruments are part of a series of norm-referenced and criterion-referenced tests (K through 12). The preprimer (K-0 through K-5) and the primer (K-5 through 1-4) levels of the test battery measure reading, mathematics, and language skills. Total administration time for the 3 subtests is approximately 1 hour and 40 minutes.

Otis-Lennon Mental Ability Test — Primary I Level

AUTHORS: Arthur S. Otis and Roger T. Lennon
DATE: 1967
SOURCE: Western Psychological Services, 12031 Wilshire Boule-

vard, Los Angeles, California 90025

AGE/GRADE: The last half of kindergarten

DESCRIPTION: This instrument is part of a series (K-12) designed to provide for comprehensive and continuous assessment of general mental ability or scholastic aptitude. Primary I level is administered in 2 separate sittings for a total testing time of 30 to 35 minutes. Fifty-five test items sample mental processes of classification, following directions, quantitative reasoning, and comprehension of verbal concepts. The test booklet contains 8 pages.

Primary Survey Test Battery: Vocabulary Survey Test

AUTHORS: Marion Monroe, John C. Manning, Joseph M. Manning

DATE: 1974

SOURCE: Scott, Foresman and Company, 1955 Montreal Road, Tucker, Georgia 30084

AGE/GRADE: Mid-kindergarten

DESCRIPTION: This instrument is part of a series of tests designed for use with K to 3rd grade children. The tests measure children's individual strengths and weaknesses in reading, spelling, language, and mathematics in order that teachers can plan appropriate instruction for each child. The Vocabulary Survey Test is the only part of the test battery administered to kindergarten children. It contains 94 items and measures strengths and weaknesses in oral vocabulary, provides clues to a child's experience, and indicates whether a child can attend to and follow directions.

Tests of Achievement in Basic Skills: Mathematics

AUTHOR: James C. Young

DATE: 1974

SOURCE: Educational and Industrial Testing Service, P. O. Box 7334, San Diego, California 92107

AGE/GRADE: Preschool and kindergarten

DESCRIPTION: This instrument is part of a series of criterion-referenced tests (K-12) designed to determine a child's achievement in math skills. The kindergarten test consists of 36 problems and is divided into 3 parts: (1) Arithmetic Skills (numeration concepts, addition, subtraction, identification of halves, thirds, and quarters); (2) Geometry-Measurement-Application (geometric shapes, length, time, money, etc.); and (3) Modern Concepts (one-to-one correspondence, inequality, odd-even concepts, etc.). An easel flip chart is used to administer the test, which is completed in 1 hour.

Tests of Achievement in Basic Skills: Reading and Language Level K

AUTHOR: Developed by EDITS
SOURCE: Educational and Industrial Testing Service, P. O. Box 7334, San Diego, California 92107
AGE/GRADE: Preschool and kindergarten
DESCRIPTION: This instrument is part of a series (K-4) of criterion-referenced tests designed to determine a child's achievement in reading and language skills. Level K consists of 4 parts: (1) Word Analysis Skills (visual discrimination, auditory discrimination, and auditory-visual discrimination skills), (2) Language Development (vocabulary, relationships, classification), (3) Comprehension (recognizing main ideas, identifying details, sequences, etc.), and (4) Study Skills (locating materials and using maps). Test booklets come in 2 parts, Reading and Language.

Category 2

PERCEPTUAL

Kerby Learning Modality Test

AUTHOR: Maude L. Kerby
DATE: 1978
SOURCE: Western Psychological Services, 12031 Wilshire Boulevard, Los Angeles, California 90025
AGE/GRADE: 5 to 11 years
DESCRIPTION: The purpose of this test is to measure strengths and weaknesses of children in the areas of vision, hearing, and motor activity. There are 8 subtests: Visual and Auditory Discrimination, Visual and Auditory Closure, Visual and Auditory Memory, and Visual and Auditory Motor Coordination. The test can be administered in 15 minutes.

Kindergarten Auditory Screening Test (KAST)

AUTHOR: Jack Katz
DATE: 1971
SOURCE: Follett Publishing Company, 1010 West Washington Boulevard, Chicago, Illinois 60607
AGE/GRADE: Kindergarten and first grade
DESCRIPTION: KAST was designed to identify children who have auditory perception difficulties. This screening test is fully recorded on one 33-1/3 RPM record and consists of three subtests: listening for speech against a background of noise, synthesizing phonemes into words, and telling whether words in pairs are the same or different. Children mark their answers in a 20-page picture response book. A group of 6 to 10 children can be tested in 20 minutes.

Mertens Visual Perception Test

AUTHOR: Marjorie K. Mertens

DATE: 1974
SOURCE: Western Psychological Services, 12031 Wilshire Boulevard, Los Angeles, California 90025
AGE/GRADE: Kindergarten through first grade
DESCRIPTION: This instrument was designed to measure the level of functioning in 6 areas of visual perception that are closely related to reading ability. The child marks his/her answers in a 16-page test booklet completed in 20 to 30 minutes. The 6 subtests are: (1) Design Copying, (2) Design Reproduction, (3) Framed Pictures, (4) Design Completion, (5) Spatial Recognition, and (6) Visual Memory.

Screening Test for the Assignment of Remedial Treatments (START)

AUTHOR: A. Edward Ahr
DATE: 1968
SOURCE: Priority Innovation, Inc., P. O. Box 792, Skokie, Illinois 60076
AGE/GRADE: 4 to 6 years
DESCRIPTION: Designed as a screening test for young children, this instrument assesses development of visual memory, auditory memory, visual-motor coordination, and visual discrimination. The test booklet contains 50 pages, one test item per page, and can be completed in one hour.

Tests of Group Learning Skills

AUTHOR: Michael A. Watson
DATE: 1976
SOURCE: Educational Activities, Inc., P. O. Box 392, Freeport, New York 11520
AGE/GRADE: 3-6 to 11 years
DESCRIPTION: This test measures 8 basic information processing skills: (1) Visual Motor, (2) Visual Memory, (3) Visual Discrimination, (4) Visual Association, (5) Auditory Memory, (6) Auditory Discrimination, (7) Auditory Association, and (8) Auditory-Visual Association. Children preschool to kindergarten ages are tested in groups of 10 to 15. Testing involves

use of cassettes for the auditory subtests and filmstrips for the visual subtests. Two to three mornings are required to complete testing.

Winter Haven Perceptual Forms Test

AUTHOR: Winter Haven Lions Club
DATE: 1955-1968
SOURCE: Winter Haven Educational Services of Winter Haven, Inc., P. O. Box 2034, Winter Haven, Florida 33880
AGE/GRADE: Kindergarten and first grade
DESCRIPTION: This test, which is part of a perceptual training program, measures visual-motor coordination by requiring the child to copy 8 geometric forms. The second part of the test involves having the child complete geometric designs that are partially drawn. The test can be administered in groups or individually and requires approximately 10 minutes to complete.

Category 3

READINESS

Analysis of Readiness Skills:
Reading and Mathematics

AUTHORS: Mary C. Rodrigues, William H. Vogler, and James F. Wilson
DATE: 1972
SOURCE: Houghton-Mifflin Company, 666 Miami Circle, N. E., Atlanta, Georgia 30324
AGE/GRADE: Kindergarten through first grade
DESCRIPTION: This test provides an index of reading and mathematics readiness by testing the child's understanding of the alphabet and of numbers. Administered in either Spanish or English, this test can be used individually or with small groups and completed in 30 to 40 minutes. The child marks his/her answers to the teacher's oral questions in an 8-page test booklet.

Circus: Sequential Tests of
Educational Progress (STEP), Level A

AUTHORS: Developed by Educational Testing Service, Princeton, New Jersey
DATE: 1974
SOURCE: Addison-Wesley Testing Service, Suite 168, 120 Interstate North Parkway, E., Atlanta, Georgia 30339
AGE/GRADE: Nursery school and beginning kindergarten
DESCRIPTION: This battery is part of a comprehensive testing program for pupils in preprimary and primary grade levels (up to grade 3). Level A consists of 14 test booklets and three teacher-completed instruments and assesses children's interests, problem solving, prereading and reading skills, mathematics concepts, and perceptual-motor coordination. Each measure requires approximately 30 minutes to administer; a core group of tests is recommended.

Clymer-Barrett Prereading Battery

AUTHORS: Theodore Clymer and Thomas C. Barrett
DATE: 1969
SOURCE: Western Psychological Services, 12031 Wilshire Boulevard, Los Angeles, California 90025
AGE/GRADE: Kindergarten through first grade
DESCRIPTION: This instrument was designed to evaluate and diagnose pupils' prereading skills and abilities in order to plan beginning reading instruction. The test can be administered in three 30-minute sessions, or a shortened screening version can be administered in one 30-minute session. Two equivalent forms are available for retest purposes.

The Contemporary School Readiness Test

AUTHOR: Clara Elbert Sauer
DATE: 1970
SOURCE: Montana Reading Publications, 1810 3rd Avenue North, Billings, Montana 59102
AGE/GRADE: End of kindergarten or during the first 3 weeks of first grade
DESCRIPTION: This test was designed to predict the success of children in the first grade and consists of 9 subtests: (1) Writing My Name, (2) Colors of the Spectrum, (3) Science, Health, and Social Studies, (4) Numbers, (5) Handwriting, (6) Reading, (7) Visual Discrimination, (8) Auditory Discrimination, and (9) Listening Comprehension. Children are tested in groups of no more than 15. Testing in the 11-page booklet is completed in 2 sessions of approximately 1 hour each.

Comprehensive Tests of Basic Skills (CTBS): Readiness Test

AUTHORS: Developed by CTB/McGraw-Hill
DATE: 1977
SOURCE: CTB/McGraw-Hill, Del Monte Research Park, Monterey, California 93940
AGE/GRADE: Kindergarten and first grade
DESCRIPTION: This instrument helps teachers determine if children have the skills necessary for beginning reading before

they actually begin formal reading instruction. The following subtests are included: Letter Names, Letter Forms, Listening for Information, Letter Sounds, Visual Discrimination, and Sound Matching. Two hours and 39 minutes are required to complete testing.

First Grade Screening Test

AUTHORS: John E. Pate and Warren Webb
DATE: 1969
SOURCE: American Guidance Service, Publishers Building, Circle Pines, Minnesota 55014
AGE/GRADE: Kindergarten through beginning first grade
DESCRIPTION: This test was designed to identify children who are likely to experience significant difficulty during the first year of school. The classroom teacher can administer the instrument to small groups of kindergarten children in 45 minutes. There are 2 forms of the 28-page test booklet, one for boys and one for girls. Each page of the test booklet contains only 1 item.

Harrison-Stroud Reading Readiness Profiles

AUTHORS: M. Lucile Harrison and James B. Stroud
DATE: 1956
SOURCE: Houghton-Mifflin Company, 666 Miami Circle, N. E., Atlanta, Georgia 30324
AGE/GRADE: Kindergarten through first grade
DESCRIPTION: The purpose of this instrument is to help teachers determine specific skills with which children may need help before or during beginning reading instruction. Five tests are included: (1) Using Symbols, (2) Making Visual Discriminations, (3) Using the Context, (4) Making Auditory Discriminations, and (5) Using Context and Auditory Clues. Tests are administered to groups of 12 to 15 children in 3 test periods of 15, 34, and 27 minutes each.

Jansky Modified Screening Index

AUTHORS: Jeanette Jansky and Katrina de Hirsch

DATE: 1973
SOURCE: The Orton Society, Inc., 8415 Bellona Lane, Towson, Maryland 21204
AGE/GRADE: 5 to 7 years
DESCRIPTION: The purpose of the Index is to identify children at risk of failing to learn to read by the end of the second grade. Subtests include letter and picture recognition, word matching, and copying figures from the Bender Visual Motor Gestalt Test. It may be administered individually or in groups and takes approximately 20 minutes.

Lee-Clark Reading Readiness Test

AUTHORS: J. Murray Lee and Willis W. Clark
DATE: 1962
SOURCE: CTB/McGraw-Hill, Del Monte Research Park, Monterey, Calfornia 93940
AGE/GRADE: Kindergarten through first grade
DESCRIPTION: This test was designed to help determine which pupils are ready for reading instruction and to establish the pattern of maturation of those not yet ready. Four subtests measure visual discrimination, recognition of differences and similarities in letter symbols, knowledge of concepts, and the pupil's ability to recognize and differentiate word symbols. The test booklet contains 10 pages and can be administered in 20 minutes. Two of the subtests have a strict 2-minute time limit.

Lippincott Reading Readiness Test

AUTHOR: Pierce H. McLeod
DATE: 1965
SOURCE: Lyons and Carnahan, Inc., 407 East 25th Street, Chicago, Illinois 60615
AGE/GRADE: Kindergarten through first grade
DESCRIPTION: This instrument consists of 2 screening devices. The Letter Knowledge Test measures the child's knowledge of printed, spoken, and written letter forms. The Readiness Checklist consists of 33 statements about the child's physical and psychological development; each statement is to be checked "yes" or "no" by the teacher. The recommended group size for

testing is 8 to 10 children. Twenty to 30 minutes is required to complete the test, which is contained in a 9-page booklet.

Metropolitan Readiness Tests

AUTHORS: Joanne R. Nurss and Mary E. McGauvran
DATE: 1976
SOURCE: Harcourt Brace Jovanovich, Inc., 757 Third Avenue, New York, New York 10017
AGE/GRADE: Kindergarten and first grade
DESCRIPTION: This test consists of 2 levels. Level I is for use with children in the first half of kindergarten and measures auditory memory, rhyming, visual skills, language skills, and copying. The 25-page test booklet requires a total of 105 minutes to complete in 7 sessions. Level II is administered during the second half of kindergarten or to first grade entrants and measures auditory skills, visual skills, language skills, quantitative skills, and copying. The 23-page test booklet requires a total of 110 minutes to complete in 5 testing sessions.

Monroe Reading Aptitude Tests

AUTHOR: Marion Monroe
DATE: 1963
SOURCE: Houghton-Mifflin Company, 666 Miami Circle, N. E., Atlanta, Georgia 30324
AGE/GRADE: Kindergarten through first grade
DESCRIPTION: The purpose of this test is to analyze 6 factors considered to be essential to success in reading (visual discrimination, auditory discrimination, motor control, oral speed, articulation, language). The group administered tests take 30 to 40 minutes and the individually administered tests take 10 to 15 minutes.

PMA Readiness Level

AUTHORS: L. L. Thurstone and Thelma Gwinn Thurstone
DATE: 1974

SOURCE: Science Research Associates, 259 East Erie Street, Chicago, Illinois 60611

AGE/GRADE: Kindergarten through first grade

DESCRIPTION: This instrument was designed to provide an assessment of mental factors associated with learning readiness; each of the 5 subtests comes in a 4-page test booklet. The subtests measure the child's verbal facility, perceptual speed, number facility, ability to perceive spatial relations, and auditory discrimination. The test is administered in two 30-minute sessions to groups of no more than 10 children.

Preschool and Early Primary Skill Survey (PEPSS)

AUTHORS: Jonh A. Long, Jr., Morton Morris, and George A. W. Stouffer, Jr.

DATE: 1971

SOURCE: Stoelting Company, 1350 South Kostner Avenue, Chicago, Illinois 60623

AGE/GRADE: 3-3 to 7-2 years

DESCRIPTION: This test was designed to measure skills significant for early school success and consists of 4 subtests: Picture Recognition, Picture Relationship, Picture Sequences, and Form Completion. There are a total of 54 items in the survey, which can be administered in 1 hour (approximately 15 minutes for each subtest).

Prescriptive Reading Inventory: Level I

AUTHORS: Developed by CTB/McGraw-Hill

DATE: 1977

SOURCE: CTB/McGraw-Hill, Del Monte Research Park, Monterey, California 93940

AGE/GRADE: Kindergarten through first grade

DESCRIPTION: This instrument is part of a criterion-referenced testing system that measures student mastery of reading objectives commonly taught in K through 6 grades. Level I contains 10 category objectives and 20 specific objectives. Prereading and initial reading behaviors are assessed in the following skill areas: Auditory Discrimination, Visual Discrimination, Alphabet Knowledge, Language Experience, Comprehension, and Attention Skills. Administered in several sessions, the test takes a total of approximately 75 minutes.

School Readiness Test

Author: O. F. Anderhalter
Date: 1975
Source: Scholastic Testing Service, Inc., 480 Meyer Road, Bensenville, Illinois 60106
Age/Grade: End of kindergarten and before third full week of first grade
Description: This test was designed to determine school readiness and consists of 7 subtests: (1) Word Recognition, (2) Identifying Letters, (3) Visual Discrimination, (4) Auditory Discrimination, (5) Comprehension and Interpretation, (6) Number Readiness, and (7) Handwriting. The 15-page test booklet is completed in two 30-minute sessions.

Screening Test of Academic Readiness (STAR)

Author: A. Edward Ahr
Date: 1966
Source: Priority Innovations, Inc., P. O. Box 792, Skokie, Illinois 60076
Age/Grade: 4 to 6 years
Description: Designed to screen preschool and kindergarten children for possible problems at an early age, this instrument consists of 50 items. There are 8 subtests: (1) Picture Vocabulary, (2) Letters, (3) Picture Completion, (4) Copying, (5) Picture Description, (6) Human Figure Drawing, (7) Relationships, and (8) Numbers. The 49-page test booklet is completed in 1 hour.

Screening Test for Auditory Comprehension of Language (STACL)

Author: Elizabeth Carrow-Woolfolk
Date: 1973
Source: Teaching Resources Corporation, 50 Pond Park Road, Hingham, Massachusetts 02043

AGE/GRADE: 3 to 6 years

DESCRIPTION: The purpose of this test is to identify children who have receptive language problems in English or Spanish. The instrument consists of 25 items that sample vocabulary, morphology, and syntax. Five to ten minutes is needed to administer.

Stanford Early School Achievement Test: Level I (SESAT)

AUTHORS: Richard Madden and Eric F. Gardner
DATE: 1970
SOURCE: Psychological Corporation, 757 Third Avenue, New York, New York 10017
AGE/GRADE: Beginning kindergarten to beginning first grade
DESCRIPTION: Level I helps teachers establish a baseline as to where experiences in school should begin by measuring what the child has already learned. The four subtests are the Environment, Mathematics, Letters and Sounds, and Aural Comprehension. One hour and 30 minutes divided over 5 testing sessions is needed to complete testing. Groups of not more than 6 or 7 children are tested at one time at the beginning kindergarten level.

Tests of Basic Experiences: Second Edition (TOBE 2)

AUTHOR: Margaret H. Moss
DATE: 1978
SOURCE: CTB/McGraw-Hill, Del Monte Research Park, Monterey, California 93940
AGE/GRADE: Preschool and first grade
DESCRIPTION: The purpose of this series of short tests is to measure how well children's experiences and concept acquisition have prepared them for participation in classroom instruction. TOBE 2 consists of 2 levels: Level K (preschool and kindergarten) and Level L (kindergarten and first grade). Each level has 4 tests: language, mathematics, science, and social studies. Approximately 25 minutes are required to administer each test.

Category 4

SOCIOEMOTIONAL

Arlin-Hills Attitude Surveys: Primary Level

AUTHORS: Marshall Arlin and David Hills
DATE: 1976
SOURCE: Publishers Test Service, 2500 Garden Road, Monterey, California 93940
AGE/GRADE: Kindergarten through third grade
DESCRIPTION: The Primary Level is part of a group of surveys (K-12) designed to assess student attitudes toward teachers, learning processes, language arts, and mathematics. Each level consists of 4 individual attitude questionnaires that require approximately 10 minutes each to complete and contain 15 items on 2 pages.

California Test of Personality: Primary Level

AUTHORS: Louis P. Thorpe, Willis W. Clark, and Ernest W. Tiegs
DATE: 1953
SOURCE: CTB/McGraw-Hill, Del Monte Research Park, Monterey, California 93940
AGE/GRADE: Kindergarten through third grade
DESCRIPTION: This instrument is part of a series of tests (K-Adult) designed to identify the status of certain personality and social adjustment factors. The test has 2 parts: Personal Adjustment (self-reliance, sense of personal worth, sense of personal freedom, feeling of belonging, withdrawing tendencies, and nervous symptoms) and Social Adjustment (social standards, social skills, anti-social tendencies, family relations, school relations, and community relations). The 8-page booklet is completed in 45 minutes.

Primary Academic Sentiment Scale (PASS)

Author: Glen Robbins Thompson
Date: 1968
Source: Priority Innovation, Inc., P. O. Box 792, Skokie, Illinois 60076
Age/Grade: 4-4 to 7-3 years
Description: The classroom teacher administers this scale to groups of 11 to 25 children in order to obtain objective information about a child's motivation for learning. The test takes 45 minutes to administer and may be given in 2 sessions. Each child receives a 38-page test booklet and is asked to look at the 3 pictures on each page and mark with a pencil the picture of the thing they would "like to do best."

The Self-Concept and Motivation Inventory (SCAMIN): What Face Would You Wear?

Authors: Norman J. Milchus, George A. Farrah, and William Reitz
Date: 1968
Source: Person-O-Metrics, Inc., 20504 Williamsburg Road, Dearborn Heights, Michigan 48127
Age/Grade: 4 to 6 years
Description: The purpose of this test (which has forms available for up to the twelfth grade) is to evaluate academic self-concept and academic motivation. The preschool form consists of 24 items and takes approximately 25 minutes to administer. The teacher describes a situation to the children and asks them "what face would you wear" in that situation. The child then marks one of three faces (frowning, neutral, smiling) on his/her score sheet.

INSTRUMENTS RECOMMENDED
FOR USE ONLY BY
CLINICIANS AND SPECIALISTS

Arthur Point Scale of Performance Tests (Grace Arthur)

Assessment in Infancy: Ordinal Scales of Psychological Development (Ina C. Uzgiris and J. McV. Hunt)

Auditory Discrimination Test (Joseph M. Wepman)

Bankson Language Screening Test (Nicholas W. Bankson)

Bayley Scales of Infant Development (Nancy Bayley)

Bender Gestalt Test for Young Children (Elizabeth M. Koppitz)

Bender Visual Motor Gestalt Test (Lauretta Bender)

Carrow Elicited Language Inventory (Elizabeth Carrow)

Cattell Infant Intelligence Scale (Psyche Cattell)

Children's Apperception Test (Leopold Bellak and Sonya S. Bellak)

Developmental Sentence Analysis (Laura L. Lee and Roy A. Koenigsknecht)

Extended Merrill-Palmer Scale (Rachel Stutsman, Philip Merrifield, and Leland Stott)

Fisher-Longemann Test of Articulation (Hilda B. Fisher and Jerilyn A. Logemann)

Fluharty Preschool Speech and Language Screening Test (Nancy B. Fluharty)

Full-Range Picture Vocabulary Test (Robert B. Ammons and Helen S. Ammons)

Gesell Developmental Schedules: Revised (Hilda Knobloch and B. Pasamanick)

Gesell School Readiness Screening Test (Frances L. Ilg, Louise Bates Ames, Jacqueline Haines, and Clyde Gillespie)

Goldman-Fristoe Test of Articulation (Ronald Goldman and Macalyne Fristoe)

Goldman-Fristoe-Woodcock Test of Auditory Discrimination (Ronald Goldman, Macalyne Fristoe, and Richard W. Woodcock

Goodenough-Harris Drawing Test (Florence Goodenough and Dale B. Harris)

Hiskey-Nebraska Test of Learning Aptitude (Marshall S. Hiskey)

Holtzman Inkblot Test (W. H. Holtzman)

House-Tree-Person Technique (John N. Buck)

Illinois Test of Psycholinguistic Abilities (ITPA) (Samuel Kirk, James McCarthy, and Winifred Kirk)

Leiter International Performance Scale (Russell G. Leiter and Grace Arthur)

McCarthy Scale of Children's Abilities (Dorothea McCarthy)

Minnesota Preschool Scale (Florence Goodenough, Katherine Maurer, and M. J. Van Wagenen)

Porteus Maze Test (Stanley D. Porteus)

Primary Visual Motor Test (Mary R. Haworth)

Psychological Evaluation of Children's Human Figure Drawings (Elizabeth M. Koppitz)

Quick Test (R. B. Ammons and C. H. Ammons)

Raven Coloured Progressive Matrices (J. D. Raven)

Rorschach Test (Hermann Rorschach)

Screening Test of Auditory Comprehension of Language (Joseph M. Wepman)

Slosson Drawing Coordination Test (Richard L. Slosson)

Southern California Perceptual Motor Tests (A. Jean Ayres)

Sprigle School Readiness Screening Test (Herbert A. Sprigle)

Stanford-Binet Intelligence Scale, Form L-M (L. M. Terman and M. A. Merrill)

System of Multicultural Pluralistic Assessment (SOMPA) (Jane R. Mercer and June F. Lewis)

Templin-Darley Tests of Articulation (Mildred C. Templin and Frederick L. Darley)

Vane Kindergarten Test (Julia R. Vane)

Wechsler Preschool and Primary Scale of Intelligence (David Wechsler)

BIBLIOGRAPHY

Buros, O. K. (Ed.): *Eighth Mental Measurement Yearbook*. Highland Park, New Jersey, Gryphon Press, 1978.

Buros, O. K. (Ed.): *Tests in Print II*. Highland Park, New Jersey, Gryphon Press, 1974.

Educational Testing Service: *Headstart Test Collection Reports*. Princeton, 1971, 1977.

Frankenburg, William K. and Camp, Bonnie W.: *Pediatric Screening Tests*. Springfield, Thomas, 1975.

Hoepfner, Ralph, Stern, Carol and Nunmedal, Susan G. (Eds.): *CSE-ECRC Pre-School Kindergarten Tests Evaluations*. Los Angeles, UCLA Graduate School of Education, 1971.

Johnson, H. Wayne: *Preschool Test Descriptions: Test Matrix Correlated Test Descriptors*. Springfield, Thomas, 1979.

Johnson, Orval G.: *Tests and Measurements in Child Development. Handbook II* (2 Vols.). San Francisco, Jossey-Bass, 1976.

Johnson, Orval G. and Bommarito, James W.: *Tests and Measurements in Child Development: A Handbook*. San Francisco, Jossey-Bass, 1971.

Mauser, August J.: *Assessing the Learning Disabled: Selected Instruments*. 2d ed. Novato, Academic Therapy Publications, 1977.

Meier, John H.: Screening, assessment and intervention for young children at developmental risk. In Hobbs, N. (Ed.): *Issues in the Classification of Children, Vol. II*. San Francisco, Jossey-Bass, pp. 497-543, 1975.

Rosen, Pamela and Horne, Eleanor V. (Eds.): *Test Collection Bulletin*. Princeton, Educational Testing Service, 1967-1978

Walker, Deborah K.: *Socioemotional Measures for Preschool and Kindergarten Children*. San Francisco, Jossey-Bass, 1974.

Wildemuth, Barbara M. (Ed.): *News on Tests*. Princeton, Educational Testing Service, 1979-1980.

Zeithin, Shirley: *Kindergarten Screening: Early Identification of Potential High Risk Learners*. Springfield, Thomas, 1976.

NAME INDEX

SUBJECT INDEX

for Preschools: The Brekken Drouin Developmental Spotcheck, 54

Orton-Gillingham approach to learning disabilities, 156

Oseretsky Test of Motor Ability, 103, 105

Otis-Lennon Mental Ability Test — Primary I Level, 168

P

Parent, as administrator, possible administrator, or primary source of information: 23, 29, 30, 33, 37, 38, 41, 43, 53, 54, 55, 59, 69, 73, 82, 84, 100, 119, 121, 122, 128, 131, 132, 147

other methods of involvement of: 24, 25, 28, 34, 37, 40, 41, 44, 46, 57, 59, 62, 65, 69, 75, 76, 100, 107, 110, 114, 135

Parent Readiness Evaluation of Preschoolers (PREP), 55

Peabody Individual Achievement Test (PIAT), 15

Peabody Picture Vocabulary Test (PPVT), 16

Perceptual Category, viii, 171-175, *see also* Visual Motor/Visual Perceptual Category

Perceptual Organization Screening Inventory, 31

Personal/Social adjustment, *see* Socioemotional Categories

Piagetian concepts, viii

instruments mentioning use of: 7, 8, 12, 18, 19, 159

PIAT, 15

Pictorial Test of Bilingualism and Language Dominance, 93

PMA Readiness Level, 178

Portage Guide to Early Education: Checklist, 57

Porteus Maze Test, *see* Clinical and specialized instruments

PPVT, 16

Pre-Academic Learning Inventory (PAL, 57

Pre-Reading Screening Procedures: Revised Edition, 156

Preschool and Early Primary Skill Survey (PEPSS), 179

Preschool and Kindergarten Performance Profile, 60

Pre-School Attainment Record (PAR). 95

Preschool Behavior Questionnaire, 139

Preschool Language Scale (PLS), 95

Pre-School Screening Instrument (PSSI), 61

Preschool Screening System: Start of a Longitudinal-Preventive Approach, 62

Preschool Screening Test, 63

Preschool Self-Concept Picture Test, 140

Prescriptive Reading Inventory: Level I, 179

Primary Academic Sentiment Scale (PASS), 183

Primary Self-Concept Inventory (PSCI), 141

Primary Survey Test Battery: Vocabulary Survey Test, 169

Primary Visual Motor Test, *see* Clinical and specialized instruments

Project Head Start, 112

Psychiatric Behavior Scale, 142

Psycho-Educational Battery (PEB), 64

Psychoeducational Evaluation of the Preschool Child, 65

Psychological Evaluation of Children's Human Figure Drawings, *see* Clinical and specialized instruemnts

Pupil Behavior Inventory (PBI): Early Education Version, 143

Pupil Record of Education Behavior (PREB), 66

Q

Quick Neurological Screening Test (QNST), 67

Quick Test, *see* Clinical and specialized instruments

R

Raven Coloured Progressive Matrices, *see* Clinical and specialized instruments

Readiness Categories, viii, ix, 106-126, 174-183, *see also* 14

Readiness for Kindergarten: A Coloring Book for Parents, 119

Reading readiness, *see* Readiness Categories, *see also* 170